Also by Scott Manley Hadley

POETRY:

Bad Boy Poet, (Open Pen, 2018)

Because Earth Is Flat: A Flat Earth Poetry Collection, (with Sean Preston,

Truther Press 2020)

PROSE:

My Father, From A Distance, (Selcouth Station, 2019)

The Pleasure of Regret, (Broken Sleep Books, 2020)

EDITOR:

SCAT TO BE POO: An Anthology of Writing About Poo (Truther Press, 2021)

HIP-HOP-O-CRIT

Hadley

ISBN: 978-1-913642-70-9

Cover design by Aaron Kent

Edited & Typeset by Aaron Kent

Broken Sleep Books (2021)

Broken Sleep Books Ltd
Rhydwen,
Talgarreg,
SA44 4HB
Wales

Contents

hip-hop-o-crit

Scott Manley Hadley

for Jane
(none of these songs are about you)

1. A Rap About Tom Jones, Scott Hadley, & Philanderers

May 13th, 2012

Lyrics:

People say I've lost it cuz I'm losing my hair,[1]
But I'm still badass, I'm still there.
I'm still fucking cool, I'm still fucking dandy,
I'm as popular now as late eighties John Candy.[2]

People say you have to be young to rap[3],
But I don't really want to have to think about that.
Cuz I make my beats at the kitchen table[4],
I mean more business than Vince fucking Cable.[5]

I live for the music, I live for the rhyme[6],
I'm a product, yeah, of my place and time.
I rap about real life and what goes on,
I read the papers, I'm fucking switched on.

Just this morning, for example, in the news
I read about a country that's running short of food.
Don't remember where it was, somewhere below the equator
But I do remember the name of the paper.

The name of the paper.[7]

[pause rapping for a few beats]

---

1   It is apt, I suppose, that even aged 23 with a full(ish) head of glorious, thick, brown hair, I was already fearing for its loss. I had an ever-higher widow's peak from the age of about 17, but I didn't shave my head until three years after this rap was recorded, when 26. The decision to become a rapper was meant to be an aggressive attempt at reasserting my own sense of youth, of potentiality, of *hope*. Even within that, though, I struggled with unfelt posturing and – crucially – opened my rap oeuvre with a line drawing attention to the thing I was most ashamed of: my early onset hair loss.

2   Who was *very* popular. Honestly, though, I wasn't.

3   As I commented above, I was 23 years old when I recorded this, but I felt *too* old, somehow. I still do.

4   100% accurate.

5   At time of rap composition and performance, Vince Cable was a British cabinet minister and member of the House of Commons, during the (now infamous) Conservative-Liberal Democrat coalition of 2010-2015. His job title was Secretary of State for Business, Innovation and Skills, and thus NO ONE in the UK "meant more business" than Vince fucking Cable. Except Hip-Scott, apparently.

6   I do not and I never have.

7   It isn't mentioned, but it would have been the Guardian online.

I come from the Midlands, suburban England,
Let me run through a bit of my personal history.[8]
Born in a small town where not much goes on,
I jumped the county line to Stratford-upon-Avon.[9]

Got my education, it served me well[10],
Learnt about Shakespeare and the Lamp[11] as well.
Did everything I could, my crossdressing[12] glory,
Then I moved to Wales, but that's a different story.

---

8   Getting cocky enough to drop the rhyme and hope no one notices, right in the second verse of my first ever rap. It's a bad look and speaks volumes about the litany of half-cocked verses I was to pen over the following few years.

9   What this means is that I passed the 11-plus and went to my achingly middle class grammar school, just outside of Stratford-upon-Avon, Warwickshire, rather than the comprehensive high school in my own hometown of Redditch, Worcestershire. That famous Worcs/Warks county line that just keeps gettin' "jumped".

10   It didn't. At time of writing these notes (fyi late Summer 2018), I am thirty years old and annotating my own rap lyrics from six years ago while sat in a tiny studio room in one of the most beautiful cities of the world, unable to afford much beyond rent except for Lidl's blesséd €1.79 cava. To be fair to myself, I'm having a great time here in Barcelona, but I don't think there are many people who would consider my adulthood as evidence of my education having "served me well". For those unaware, my adulthood has mostly (so far) been spent as a millionaire's depressed male mistress, but since I lost that job I've been an underemployed dilettante poet slash English-as-a-foreign-language tutor slash dog owner slash occasional copywriter. I've had adventures, yes, but I am not what anyone – except my dog – would call a *success*.

11   What this means is that the previous line may **actually** have been more knowing than I'd presumed, because the Lamplighter (or, as we affectionately called it, "The Lamp") was the pub we used to drink in, underage, in Stratford-upon-Avon. Maybe I'm alluding to my education serving only to teach me how to rely on intoxication to drown my feelings? Maybe not, though: I don't think I was very wise to myself aged 23.

12   I would get back into "crossdressing", i.e. drag, in a big way when a little older. (Note from late Summer 2020: At time of writing *this* note, I identify as non-binary whenever I have the option to do so on a form, but I'm scared to inhabit a non-cis identity publicly because I read so bluntly as "man" to strangers and I fear confrontation over something that matters so much. I'm a very masculinised person (slightly above average height, bald, stocky due to being overweight), though I do frequently wear jumpsuits and patterned clothes, neither of which are standard for "men" here in Toronto, where people dress far more conservatively than in London and Barcelona. Every time I'm asked to provide pronouns in a real-life setting, though, I have a panic attack, which I'm good at doing silently now. I recently bought a lovely, flattering, plain, dress to wear, but it's been wrapped up since I tried it on (and felt spectacular) because I'm too scared of the risk of abuse if I were to wear it outside. I don't feel comfortable in my body, at all, at all, at all, but I don't feel comfortable doing anything to change that feeling, other than regularly doing cardio while watching prestige television shows, which I suppose must be keeping me from being even fatter and even more repulsive to myself. I come from a fat family and I don't want to look like them, it makes me sick to think of doing anything in my life like them. Oh, also, in the interval between writing the majority of the notes here and the scattered few from 2020, I have been diagnosed with Borderline Personality Disorder, which explains a lot and perhaps contributes to my fraught feelings around gender and sexuality, too. For a long time I thought I was bisexual but very, very repressed, and then I thought I *wasn't* bisexual but very, very repressed: I was just heterosexual but ashamed of eroticising female bodies so wished I wasn't; but in hindsight (as an older, wiser, individual), I now think I was right the first time. There's a poem about this in Appendix A.)

Not a fan of rugby so it's kinda hard,
To visit the pubs there without getting barred[13].
So I turned my attention to something even less like home,
And became a huge fucking fan of Sir Tom fucking Jones.[14]

[incompetent guitar solo with mumbled, spoken, criticisms of it]

Born in Pontypridd in 1940,
He's currently a judge on *The Voice* on TV.
His real name is Thomas John Woodward,
He's like a Welsh Elvis but without the big stomach.

He can dance like a bitch[15], he can sing like a god,
He loved the ladies, he shagged around like a dog[16].
Used to play Las Vegas for a month every year,
He's also a boozer, he loves to drink beer.[17]

---

13   This isn't true, because the Welsh are usually very friendly, even the rugby types. (Note from Summer 2020: I remember writing a note here about the normalcy of racism in Wales, but as I didn't spend enough time in Wales *more broadly* to know if Welsh racism was widespread or just a problem with the [vast majority of the] Welsh people *who chose to study in Cardiff*, I deleted it. For example, a woman I knew from the student drama society (yes, I was in the student drama society) had a birthday cake – I'm not making this up – that was "concentration camp" themed. Like, decorated with barbed wire, nails and a miniature "Arbeit Macht Frei" sign. That's pretty fucking extreme racism, I suppose, though knowing one very racist Welsh person and extrapolating outwards about *all* Welsh people is the kinda thing it is churlish to do. I am more than happy, though, to make sweeping judgements about the English as I'm "allowed" to do that and I frequently do both on my blog *TriumphoftheNow.com* and on Twitter, where I can be found and followed at @Scott_Hadley. This generalising about the English happens more than once in the remainder of this text.)

14   The majority of the rest of this song is about Tom Jones, the Welsh pop singer.

15   Uncertain what "a bitch" dances like, and I do not stand by this use of language or imagery in the work of my younger self. But I won't censor it because otherwise how will people understand the *positive* ways society (and Scott Manley Hadley) has changed since May 2012.

16   My dog, Cubby, has no balls (due to deliberate castration, not heart-breaking accident) so I have no personal experience of dealing with horny dogs, except the occasional ones who try and hump my little Tibetan terrier. (Note from Summer 2020: that was a big problem in Barcelona, but wasn't an issue at all in London and hasn't been much of an issue here in Toronto, a city where people have a weird love-hate relationship with dogs that comes from that very North American fear of germs, a societal fear that seemed to evaporate as soon as it became useful. NB: does the cultural germaphobia of settler society in Canada and the USA come from the fact that people here don't forget that bacterial warfare was one of the tools used methodically (both by accident and design) against indigenous peoples as part of the colonisation of the [lands known as the] Americas? People remember that germs can help to commit genocide and are thus hyper cautious? Colonisers forever fearing the retribution in kind from those they displaced/destroyed?)

17   "Beer" is intentionally mispronounced so that it rhymes with "year". Fucking bizarre choice.

A few years ago he stopped dying his hair,
Tom is now a silver fox[18], umm umm yeah[19].
I could go on for hours, spitting rhymes about Tom[20],
But, unlike his wife, I think it's time to move on.

[more competent guitar solo, accompanied by a "dance solo"][21]

See what I mean, I'm rapping about issues,
If I've upset you, here's a box of tissues.[22]
Dry your eyes, get back in the room,
Tom's infidelity doesn't fill the world with gloom.

When he cheats on his wife, it's kinda fine,
Because he's been doing it for years and she doesn't really mind.
She once threw vodka bottles at his head,
And beat him up, so she gives and she gets.

It's not that I'm condoning his terrible behaviour,
You just can't reign in a famous philanderer.[23]

[spoken:] I thought that'd rhyme, I really thought that'd rhyme.[24]

---

18   From a young age, I dreamed of being a silver fox myself. I think it was because, on a deeply subconscious level, I always knew I was destined to be bald.

19   This is, possibly throughout Hip-Scott's entire oeuvre, the laziest rhyming couplet.

20   At no point in my life would this statement have been true.

21   Though I am now terrified by how thin my 2012 *arms* were, I do envy the shape of the lithe body under its clothes. So *boylike*. No, not so boylike: so *androgynous*. (Note from Summer 2020: I remember saying to a friend – and meaning – that I wanted to be so thin you couldn't tell my gender from the side. Now, I would know to use the word "sex" rather than gender there, but the same statement holds true. I hate being bald. I hate being fatter than I used to be, even though I exercise now. I hate my body. It sickens me. I hate looking like a *man*. I hate being addressed as a *man*. I hate hate hate hate myself. Again, see Appendix A.)

22   In the video, there appears a still image of a marketing photograph of a box of tissues, rather than a real-life prop.

23   The six lines preceding this imply a weird and skewed morality where I excuse *both* direct domestic violence and unsanctioned infidelity, by virtue of them cancelling each other out. I was a *young* 23. Now, I am an old, bald, 30.

24   Clearly this "ad lib" serves as a replacement for a couplet that the younger me couldn't be arsed to write.

As for me, I'm nothing like that,[25]
Even when I try to rap I'm no babe magnet.
I've got my books and I've got my coffee,
I'd rather read the Guardian than shag a Miss World hottie.[26]

Maybe I don't have the urge, don't have the eye,
I'd probably rather eat a pizza than stroke a sexy thigh[27].
But bodies like Tom's, they come from the ground,
He's more organic, is the man that shags around.[28]

His urges are animalistic, and so are Tom's songs,
If I did more shagging, could I SING LIKE TOM JONES???[29]

---

25   The song implies, at least in its focus, that a part of me very much *wanted* to be like that.
26   I'd like to be able to call BS on myself here, but I think that at that stage in my life I was very much *scared* of sex, it was something I didn't feel comfortable doing and, as such, avoided aggressively. I am one of the few men I know who has turned down more potential lovers than he has thrusted up. I say "few", I mean only.
27   This is why I no longer have the woefully thin body I'm shaking in the video to this rap: it turns out that pizza *does* taste as good as skinny feels.
28   I wrote my undergraduate dissertation on *Lady Chatterley's Lover* and you can tell you can tell you can tell.
29   No.

Video notes:

The video switches between many shots – some where I'm attempting to lip-sync, badly – of me around the Islington townhouse I lived in for almost seven years. There are also cutaways to still images pilfered from the internet, usually of Tom Jones. There are lots and lots of cuts and I clearly put much, untrained, effort into editing. Not the worst video of the oeuvre.

Performance Notes:

The rapping is often unclear, but I do not get ahead of myself. Hip-Scott doesn't *try* to rap faster than he can, which means this is actually a tad *too slow* a lot of the time. Still, there's no hint of a faux-American accent (which was a conspicuous feature in my pre-rap song recordings, for example 'Waste Paper'[30] (available at: https://youtu.be/C2BOkFDG5kU[31]), a song about Hannibal Lecter as a young man and Frank DuBois[32], a real life young man who I was briefly in love with), and the second guitar solo makes me sound briefly competent. What a treat!

---

30   Below is a screenshot from the video. There is a glass of red wine in my right hand, a tiny umbrella in my left and I and my first guitar are leaning on a street sign about 300m from my childhood home, where my ailing parents and my sister remain living to this day.

31
32   (Note from Summer 2020: For more on my fraught, confused, relationship with Frank DuBois, see the opening essay of *the pleasure of regret* (Broken Sleep Books, 2020).)

Track Rating:

4/5 – 'A Rap About Tom Jones, Scott Hadley & Philanderers' does everything it sets out to do: it establishes the themes (sexual repression, disgust of and disappointment in my body (though here without its usual accompaniment of exhibitionism)), establishes the aesthetic (lo-fi hip-hop and videos with no impressive shots and poor cohesion). It is a classic Hip-Scott song and very much worth the time and effort put into it. In fact, it's *so good*, that it justifies a novella-length exploration of the entirety of Hip-Scott's output.[33]

---

33   That is an opinion from which I will *not back down*.

2. I'm A Rapper

September 30th, 2012

Lyrics:

[Chorus:]   *I'm A Rapper*
Yes, I'm a mother-fucking rapper[34]

I'm A Rapper
Yes, I'm a mother-fucking rapper

I'm A Rapper
Yes, I'm a mother-fucking rapper

I'm A Rapper
Yes...
I'm a mother-fucking rapper.

I'm a fresh new rapper, I'm new to the scene,
I'm the unrecyclable plastic sheathing your fave magazine.[35]
I don't glamorise drugs, guns or women,[36]
What's that, you say, then how do I write hip-hop lyrics?

---

34   You can't argue with it. I rap, therefore I am... a rapper.

35   A "wrapper" – "rapper" pun, like all the greats use.

36   In 2012, this was the kind of thing that peopled joked about. The subject of the joke is *intended to be* me and my naïve understanding of misogyny in rap music. Of course, "glamorising women" is not the same as "objectifying women" and back in 2012 – before the rise of incels and the alt-right more generally – as a "liberal" man, I felt comfortable making this joke, which relied on the listener *understanding* that "obviously" Hip-Scott knows the difference between objectification and glamorisation. But in the world we now live in, this *wouldn't* be presumed, and this is the probably the kind of lyric some incel prick would say without irony. It is *good* that *people who don't hate women* no longer feel comfortable *pretending to hate women* for a joke, but the reason why it's utterly unacceptable is the skyrocketing popularity of genuine misogyny, which is not good for anyone. I'm sorry.

Well, my rap style's mature, my rap style is grown-up,
I drink my squash out of crystal, not out of plastic.[37]
I'm so old, I don't even go to school,[38]
That's right, I'm an adult, fool.

I'm mature like wine, I don't smell like cheese,
My lyrics bring the penitent up off their knees,
Cuz they think I'm the brand new rap messiah,
Cuz I spit rhymes more fiery than a funeral pyre.

I'm angry, I'm sharp, I'm lyrically gifted,
You can see the gold in my rap without having to sift it,[39]
Have a listen, yeah, to the beats that I got,
There's no one more fucking hip-hop than Hip-fucking-Scott.

[repeat chorus]

Don't make a lot of love, don't make a lot of war[40]
If I did more of either, it would be to a hip-hop score.
Cuz I rap when I wake up, I rap in my sleep,
I even rap when I'm cleaning the gold on my teeth.[41]

---

37   Hip-Scott is here trying to imply an immaturity in contrast to the claim of "maturity" in the previous line. Hip-Scott drinks from crystal – like a fancypants adult – but he's still drinking squash (cordial), like an English child.

38   (Note from Summer 2020: Less than six months after this, I would begin the process of applying for MA programmes. I was offered places at King's College London and Goldsmiths, University of London and selected the Creative Writing course at the latter, rather than the more analytical course at the former. In hindsight, this was a mistake, as the course did nothing at all to improve my writing (if anything it made it slightly more pretentious for a bit (compare Appendices B and C)), I've never had a "graduate job" and I only remain in occasional contact with *one person* from my course. Maybe if I was still in London, this wouldn't be the case. Actually, I'm being disingenuous, the two longer pieces I wrote in Blake Morrison's Life Writing seminars have both been published and were well-received, lol (one, titled *My Father, From A Distance*, was published as a chapbook by Selcouth Station Press in 2019, while another 'my mother, from a distance' appears in my 2020 prose collection, *the pleasure of regret*). The course wasn't "a waste of time" per se, but the more academic course at the more prestigious university might have pushed my life in a more *intellectually* satisfying direction.)

39   This line always makes me think of the bit in Legoland Windsor in the 1990s where you could pan for fools' gold like a Wild West prospector. If that's still there and you have a child under ten, why not go? Actually, don't bother, it's probably less fun than the internet *and* quite expensive. Just buy them a cheap tablet instead and put Google Safe Lock on. I don't have children, but if I did I wouldn't neglect them like I have just recommended others do. I walk my dog at least three times every day.

40   I've never made *any* war and, as we've discussed already, I am no Casanova.

41   I don't have a single filling. I also have never rapped in my sleep or while cleaning my teeth. Have definitely rapped almost immediately after waking up, though.

Some people try to tell me that I'm rapping too much,[42]
Well you people, you can just fuck off:
Rapping for me is like breathing for you,
It's not a hobby it's something that I *have to do*.

Probably rather chop my balls off than give it up,
Who in their right mind prefers children to hip-hop?[43]
My raps are a gift to the whole fucking world,
Everyone's talking about them, haven't you heard?

From London to Paris, from Brooklyn to Compton,
The famous faces of rap know there's a new star coming.
Will.i.am[44] called me up, he said, "We like what you got,
There's no one more fucking hip-hop than Hip-fucking-Scott."

[repeat chorus]

How many raps have I got within me?
Well, so far it's only been three,[45]
There're so much more hip-hop for me to give,
Get ready with a bucket cuz my lyrics are sick.

---

42   This isn't true: most people I know *ignored* my raps, rather than actively discouraging them. Sometimes, though, apathy is worse than contempt. (Note from Summer 2020: I can't believe I forgot about this. Once, at a house party or in a bar somewhere in East London during my halcyon year as a bartender-slash-creative-writing-student, a Swedish man I'd never met before came up to me and said, "Oh my god! Are you Hip-Scott?" It turned out he wasn't a complete stranger, he was friends with a different Swedish man, named Jakob, who I worked with at the time, who had played 'I'm A Rapper' to him at – I imagine – a wonderfully drug-fuelled party some time. It's one of those few moments in my life when I've ever felt certain I existed in the minds of others when they weren't with me. Jakob, btw, was very handsome and everyone on the staff fancied him, to varying degrees. Briefly, another Swede worked with us (a young woman, between semesters of a university course) and she would, every weekend, laugh at the fawning stares from staff and customers towards Jakob. "I don't understand why you're excited," she'd say, genuinely confused, "In Sweden he's just an average-looking guy."

43   I think most people, given the choice, would choose children over hip-hop. Though the sick dystopia that would force this decision on its public doesn't bear thinking about.

44   I deliberately picked an underwhelming rapper. I considered saying Mel B, but had I at that point in my life known 'Wham! Rap!' as well as I now do, I would have said Andrew Ridgely.

45   In between these two tracks I also recorded and released a covers medley, however that (obvs) contained no original lyrics so is not worth analysing.

Every time I rhyme, it's like a mental explosion,
Everyone's going mad with a Christ-like[46] devotion,
I'm just a rapper, guys, cool it all down,
I can't help being the most badass man in all London town.[47]

But don't despair, with practice you can be like me,
I'd never rapped until I was twenty-three.
And now I'm so fucking fly I feel like a Boeing,
I'm touching the sky like it got money owing.[48]

My raps are gorgeous, I'm spitting fresh magic,[49]
To continue with planes, I'm like Virgin Atlantic.[50]
My mouth's getting scalded, my raps are so hot,
There's no one more fucking hip-hop than Hip-fucking-Scott.

[repeat chorus]

[repeat chorus]

[repeat chorus]

[recorder solo]

[repeat chorus]

[synthesiser continues as I perform a weird kick to camera]

---

46   Second messianic reference in this rap, which is troubling. (Note from Summer 2020: somewhat odd that I didn't make the connection earlier, but when, during 2013 and 2014, I attempted to write a "popular" novel, one of its peripheral characters was a sex-positive, humanist Jesus who was based on an idealised version of myself. He spoke with my voice and used my mannerisms, at least those I used in my own head in private. See Appendix C.)

47   I wasn't and I knew I wasn't. The posturing arrogance of some of these raps surprises me, from a distance, as I in no way *felt* this self-confidence in my day-to-day life. Maybe that was why I *needed* the rapping, to give myself a space to pretend to feel feelings I wish I felt. Hip-Scott could be the man that younger Scott Manley Hadley could not. Luckily, the Scott Manley Hadley of 2018 is a better man than Hip-Scott could ever have become. (The Scott Manley Hadley of 2020 has not decided on his value compared to previous iterations of self.)

48   I think this line is plagiarised, but I don't know where from. The implication is that a loan shark would "touch" someone who had money owing by beating them up, and Hip-Scott is "so fucking fly" he is *touching the sky like it got money owing*. He's not just stratospheric, he's stratospheric and he's bringing the thunder, like Thor.

49   I'm not.

50   I think of Virgin Atlantic as the most luxurious airline, because they're investing in SPACE TRAVEL.

[synthesiser continues as I shout, off beat, "I'm A Rapper" at the top of a hill]

[synthesiser continues as a car beeps its horn at me as I dance beside a road]

Video notes:

Mainly shot on location in the small village of Sambourne[51], Warwickshire, the video consists of me rapping on the streets, in fields, or behind my sister's parked car while I pretend to play a boot(aka "trunk")-mounted keyboard. The lip-synching is better here than elsewhere, and the smaller range of shots makes for a more cohesive piece.

Performance Notes:

A cracking beat, a wonderful recorder solo, some tight and witty lyrics. Almost every line is perfectly enunciated, or as near-to-perfectly-enunciated as Hip-Scott was ever to get. Top track.

Track Rating:

I may have a slight bias, but for me this is absolutely *one of the all-time best songs*. 5/5. I'll be rapping this to myself in the shower until I get dementia. Or write a better rap.

---

51   A family member who doesn't like me (ikr, what's not to like???) once stumbled across this video and, after describing it as "filth", seemed personally offended that I had filmed it (and this is not misquoting) "in Sambourne, of all places".

3. Credentials

November 18th, 2012

Lyrics:

[chorus]   *I've got rap credentials,*
Where most other people just have rap genitals.[52]

I've got rap credentials,
Where most other people just have rap genitals.

I've got rap credentials,
Where most other people just have rap genitals.

I've got rap credentials,
Where most other people just have rap genitals.

Rap credential number one, is where I'm fucking from,
I'm not from the countryside as many people seem to presume,
I'm from an urban shithole, dealers and whores on every street,[53]
Armed fucking car jackings every single night of the week.[54]

Dead bodies in ditches[55], paedos running schools[56],
Teen pregnancies[57], knifings, shit tags on every wall.[58]
Station only goes to Birmingham[59], no connections, no Waitrose[60],
No prospects, a town in its fucking death throes.[61]

---

52   One of this song's biggest weaknesses – aside from the complete abandonment of form later on – is the meaninglessness of its chorus.

53   I don't believe I ever saw a soliciting prostitute or an in-transaction drug deal in my hometown, though there definitely would have been some of both there, as it was a normal English town in the '90s and we ("the English") are a nation of secret shaggers who are mad for getting wasted.

54   Again, I don't have any memory of this happening in my hometown. Hip-Scott is being dishonest…

55   Vague memories of this happening, though.

56   This one was definitely a real scandal in Redditch in the mid-1990s. It was a church-affiliated school that my sister would *later* attend. Very trusting of my parents, though, believing the "one bag egg" apology issued by the local Catholics!

57   One year in the 1990s the local high school had the highest teen pregnancy rate in Europe. NB: not the school run by a sex offender.

58   There *was* a lot of lacklustre graffiti, but "every wall" is a stretch.

59   Redditch is a post-industrial satellite town of Birmingham, so this is sadly accurate. The trainline previously (long before I was born) went in two directions, but the Southbound tracks were dismantled as part of Dr. Beeching's cuts.

60   I grew up thinking Sainsbury's was an unaffordable luxury brand. That is probably the most telling and revealing comment I have made so far.

61   (From Summer 2020: I **did not** give myself enough credit for rhyming "death throes" with "Waitrose", which is surely worthy of a prize or two.)

So urban degradation, not verdant fucking fields,
A town with five McDonalds and not a single Strada[62],
I'm urban as fuck me, so please don't forget it.
Or I'll kick you in the gutter and knife your fucking brains in.

The violence, just verbal, I'd never enact that,[63]
Credential number two: I'm all talk, no trousers.[64]
With my pants filled up with my giant fucking cock
There's no room for an Uzi or a mother-fucking Glock.[65]

Clearly I'm not involved in organised crime,[66]
I lack both the desire and the time,
I'm also short of the right connections,
Which is the same reason I always lost student elections.[67]

Credential three is where it starts to get serious,
I'm fed up with people telling me I'm being delirious,
To think that I can turn myself into a motherfucking rap star,
Just look at me, I've already come pretty motherfucking far.[68]

---

62   In 2016 or 2017 an ASK Pizza opened. Not certain on the number of McDonalds now, and though it's fewer than at its peak, there are still multiple "Maccy Ds".

63   Obviously. Though I was violently mugged within a week of moving to London in 2010, the only time I have ever been violent myself was when I punched a boy I went to school with in the face after he pulled my underwear down during a P.E. lesson on a **very** cold day. His name was [name redacted], and he wanders into my thoughts most days and I often wonder if he thinks of me as much as I think of him, and then I hope he doesn't because it would be *even weirder* if the concern was mutual. In the unpublished novel I wrote in my early twenties (*White Lines, Black Truffles*), he appears **with name unchanged** as a minor character. See Appendix B. (Note from Summer 2020: I was very discreet here before, but one of the many women who I refused to have sex with in my first year of university is, now, [name redacted]'s long-term partner. We made out at the drama society summer ball and she took me back to her apartment, where she tried to undress me and I got shy. I put my hands in her pants but wouldn't let her put hers in mine. Sometimes I'm angry at my younger self for the fun I denied myself.)

64   This phrase is usually used to mean that a man has a small penis, however the next line goes on to *brag* about the size of my penis. To be honest, my penis *is* slightly larger than average, but I hadn't quite come to terms with that at this stage in my life, but I just felt it was a strong, typisch, hip-hop lyric.

65   These are both guns, but I have no idea how big either is. I would imagine that if a gun is too big to fit into trousers, it doesn't *matter* how big your penis is. I don't know, though, I have never held a gun, let alone against my penis. (2020 note: Again, a *great* couplet.)

66   Self-knowledge: I know I don't look like a career criminal. I don't think I watched *Breaking Bad* until after the date of performance, so I had no idea of the potentiality for the moral collapse of boring, nerdy, depressed men in unhappy relationships.

67   At the end of my penultimate year of university, I stood to be treasurer of the student drama society and I comfortably lost. In high school, I was the joint runner-up to be Deputy Head Boy, though managed to scrape a title as Head of House, whatever that meant. I just wanted to feel accepted. I always felt lonely in crowds. (note from 2020: this is a v typisch Borderline Personality Disorder trait.)

68   I hadn't "come pretty motherfucking far": I have *still* never performed rap live, I have never had a record contract and nor have I pursued one. When I wrote that lyric I had recorded three original raps (including this one) and performed one covers medley on YouTube. That's not "far", by anyone's standard. I also don't think I ever believed I could be a "motherfucking rap star", and if I ever *did* believe that, I *was*

30

What's to stop a continued march on the pop charts,
Albums, singles, chat shows, concerts?[69]
They say the most important thing is the drive,
And – strangely -- I can legally drive.[70]

I don't know if that translates absolutely,
But seems like more than a coincidence to me,
My big rapper balls are primed to rap-jaculate.
Or ej-rapulate.[71] [pause]

[chorus]

[spoken]

See, I'm a badass.[72] Why I didn't move into rap, into this urban fucking
poetry[73] at an earlier date isn't clear to me, it's a mystery.

It suits me perfectly in its self-aware, self-indulgence[74] – cuz I know I'm a
hip-hop-o-crit[75]: I don't condone drugs, but nor do I refuse them.[76]

I'm a borderline[77] social recluse, yet I'm happy to put my fucking arse on
YouTube three times a year, I get immense amounts of joy and pleasure
from singing and making shit music, but I tell myself I shouldn't because
nobody wants to hear it.[78]

But fuck that, fuck that voice in my head, that *vice* in my head - the vice of
self-hatred.

---

being delirious. (Summer 2020 note: I performed three songs live at the launch of my first book, *Bad Boy Poet*, in November 2018. Since then, however, I have also done no more live rapping. Maybe I would have built towards doing so if 2020 hadn't been the nightmare that it has been (there is a global pandemic).)

69   Effort and talent.

70   To give credit to my younger, more depressed but less financially unstable, self, this is a satisfying Shakespearean pun, because, yes, people *do* cite "drive" as essential to success in the arts, and by that point in my life I did indeed have a *licence* to drive, like James Bond.

71   I'm sorry, I'm sorry, I'm sorry. This is crude nonsense.

72   No, I'm not.

73   Here's 24-year-old white English literature graduate Scott Manley Hadley describing rap as "urban fucking poetry". This is offensive and I apologise.

74   If this text was a 2,000 word essay, it could have been described as "self-aware self-indulgence". As a book of over 100 pages, though, "self-aware" would be a very, very, self-indulgent way to describe *hip-hop-o-crit*. Yes, there's a lot of this left. Strap in!

75   I remember being very, very smug about this word. AND OMG IT'S THE TITLE OF THE BOOK!!!

76   Obviously I refuse marijuana, because I don't want to feel like I'm having a cocaine comedown at like 4.30pm without having had any previous fun.

77   (Summer 2020: The psychiatrists said I'm a borderline something, too.)

78   Still to this day.

We're all *who we fucking are*, and we should express ourselves as, how and when we want to.[79]

I've come straight outta the slums[80] of fucking Worcestershire, via South Wales and... err... Angel Islington[81] to perform this for you tonight and let me tell you, I am having a fucking blast, I am having the time of my life, because – and I've told you this before – I'm a rapper, I'm a motherfucking rapper[82], I'm a legal driver, if I spend enough fucking time on the edits I could even comfortably describe myself as a novelist by the end of the year.[83]

And these things, these things that... that... spring joy into a life don't come by sitting in a corner of the room talking about what we want to be and who we want to be and where we want to be, they come from fucking standing up, sealing the bottle, putting out the spliff,[84] whatever, and going forward and doing and getting what you want.

And you can tell that to the fucking feds, and you can tell that to the fucking record labels and to fucking *Top of the Pops* magazine.[85]

Do what you enjoy.

Fucking live the life you want to live. Because you only get one. And in this one -- I'm a fucking rapper.

---

79   Very #inspiration.

80   I didn't grow up rich, nor in a slum.

81   The three places I had lived by that point in my life. Later on, during my accidental period of couchsurfing, I lived in Wapping, Limehouse, Plaistow, Dulwich, Balham and Stoke Newington, before then spending extended periods in Loughborough Junction and Seven Sisters. At the time of first drafting these notes I am in Barcelona, where I spent the majority of 2018, my *anno victoria*. (By Summer 2020 I'm in Toronto, Ontario.)

82   Reference to the previous Hip-Scott release, 'I'm A Rapper'.

83   I have written multiple unpublished novel-length manuscripts. Does that make me a novelist? No: I'm a rapper. The particular novel I'm referring to here is *White Lines, Black Truffles*, a second-person Catholic-cocaine novel that has, since this date, had a few extracts published online. Find all the links at www.scottmanleyhadley.com and see Appendix B for the chapter that imagines re-meeting [name redacted], the only man I have (to date) punched in the face.

84   Trying to sound more badass than I am, but also implying that all hip-hop fans are into marijuana, which is *again* offensive. I told a lie in the earlier footnote and, recently, I **did** accept an offer of some marijuana – while sober – out of a genuine curiosity in case I'd been wrong about it for years. My initial hypothesis was correct, though: I can confirm that marijuana is absolutely as shit as I remembered it being.

85   Every rapper's three biggest enemies.

Video Notes:

The video comprises a slew of shots recorded during a daytrip to Brighton (possibly alone, I do not remember), alternating with video footage recorded direct from the camera on my laptop as I "lay down" the vocal track. By the end I look tired, even though the delivery conspicuously shifts from rapping to expressive poetic performance.

The opening shot is the slow, zooming out, image of the wreckage of the burnt pier off the coast of Brighton beach, which cuts to a slightly skewed (presumably due to filming via a camera propped up on the beach) shot of a young Scott Manley Hadley. His gorgeous, thick, brown hair pokes out from beneath a red and white woollen hat that has "James Bond" knitted into it.[86] The best bit of the video is the close up shots of my – for want of a better word – *breath-taking* – 24-year-old arse.

Performance Notes:

Far too much slurring during *too many* lines of the rap, there are more lost words during *this* track than both of the previous pieces. The spoken word section at the end is more competently performed, but it lacks a *feeling* of immediacy, it is *very clearly* not an adlib. Musically, though, it is one of Hip-Scott's most accomplished tracks, especially the section that follows the second chorus that uses the synth vibrato glockenspiel from a children's keyboard in combination with a heavily treated melodic scream.

---

86   This hat, I suppose, is significant, and it hasn't cropped up in my recent work about myself and my life in the way that it should have. It was knitted by hand by my former partner, early in the very long relationship that was, for more than 50% of its length, very, mutually, unhappy. "Toxic" is the word people use. This hat was probably the final gift she gave me while there was still a semblance of love. After that – and before, too – she mainly gave me gifts that I didn't understand, by designers so elite that their clothes didn't resemble anything I'd seen before. I once mentioned in passing that I liked the look of leather jackets (despite being a vegetarian), and then she bought me a Missoni suede, slimcut jacket with woollen embroidery on the back and I was like, "wow, it's so kooky, what is it?" and she was like "it's fucking Missoni, it was fucking expensive, you said you wanted a leather jacket and this is suede which is leather" but it didn't make me look like a tough biker or a member of the Village People (both of which I'd've liked), it instead just made me look like someone who had access (well, proximity) to money and took cocaine every weekend.

Track Rating:

2/5 – the performance and a vague lyrical puerility lets down a Hip-Scott track that, sadly, had the potential to be better. Musically, this is one of my most ambitious and least lazy, having composed – and performed on a guitar – both a riff and a chorus structure. The piece drops its attempts at rap for its final verse, and becomes rather uplifting and positive in a way that Hip-Scott – and my work more generally – failed to do right through until my 2018 book of poetry, *Bad Boy Poet*[87]. It's pleasing to see a younger me more optimistic, but sad to know how quickly all that hope and optimism would turn to DUST.

87

4. YouTube Celebrity
(I'll Never Be A)

February 24th, 2013

Lyrics:

[sung]

All I, all I, ever wanted to be
Was a minor YouTube celebrity.[88]
All I, all I, ever wanted to have
Was a million YouTube hits in the bag.

But my comedy sketches lacked the wit,[89]
My music the skills requisite
To capture the hearts and the minds of the internet[90],
I'll never be most viewed, I'll never be editor's pick.

[chorus]:   *I'll never be a YouTube celebrity* [x 4]
              [as chorus repeats there is some "skatting" using the
              words of the chorus]

[rapped]

So I'm sat, where I always have,
My teenage bedroom, back at my ma and dad's.
Tryna work out where the YouTube career went so wrong,
I've been at it so long now success must be near.

---

88   When I was 10, I won a competition to present the weather on BBC Midlands Today (the BBC local news in the West Midlands). At the end of the weather forecast, they had me sit on the end of the newsreaders' desk and get teasingly questioned by star newsreader Nick Owen (a once-National figure who had come down in the world) and whoever his sidekick was that evening. They asked 10-year-old, pre-pubescent, nerdy, Scott Manley Hadley what he wanted to be when he grew up, and I told them "an actor or an author". I didn't know what I meant by that then, but it was the dual aim that persisted through my teenage years, and the literary part even made it through my theatrical-experimentation-filled undergraduate years. In short, "being a YouTube celebrity" was *never* "all I ever wanted to be".

89   Find my YouTube channel via www.scottmanleyhadley.com and look at my younger self's attempts at comedy. It's not funny.

90   There's one thing you can say about unworthy people getting internet-famous, which is that – when it happens to musicians - they can do AT LEAST ONE THING incredibly well. Or so badly and earnestly that it goes viral. Hip-Scott's work is unexcitingly underwhelming.

But that's not how it works, don't be so naïve, Scott
People may love hip-hop but they don't love Hip-Scott[91]
They complain my sketches are too derivative[92]
I make them more avant garde[93] but then they're "not amusing"[94].

I listen to my critics, yeah, I adapt and repeat,
When you make a funny, I remember to retweet.[95]
Come on, World Wide Web, I give you more than enough.
Where are my online arselicks? Where is my online love?

There's this fantasy I have, I wake, glance at my phone.
A million emails from YouTube telling me what's going on:
Video replies, likes, thumbs ups, shares and comments,
The world interacting with my original content.

I walk down the street, people point and say,
"Is that the guy who-", their friend nods, already thinking the same.
"Hey, he's a rapper"[96], "I heard he's a prostitute"[97],
"That's a poor taste joke he should probably remove from the internet."[98]

---

91   Rhyming my own name with my own name, an act of self-aggrandisement never surpassed in my oeuvre until the "text" you are currently reading.

92   No one ever said this to me, but I never really put enough time into trying to do comedy sketches to *find* a "voice" of my own. Some friends of mine who I used to sometimes play funnies with when an undergraduate are doing quite well as a Welsh sketch group now. They're called the Death Hilarious, they're funny, look 'em up. (Summer 2020 note: The Death Hilarious disbanded, one of them unwilling to continue committing the time, energy and (I imagine) money required to pursue a career in the Arts. The other persists, continuing to perform under the name of their previous double act, which I think is strange but I can understand from a marketing perspective. He's good friends with the last winner of the Edinburgh Comedy Award and performed in a sketch on Channel 4 with him recently, so the career isn't over yet. His name is Darren, I miss him. I suppose I had a bit of a crush on him, too, for a long while. He's a *very sexual being*, though I think he's *very* heterosexual.)

93   Again, find my YouTube channel via www.scottmanleyhadley.com and see how "avant garde" my younger self's "avant garde" comedy sketches are. They're not avant garde.

94   I make air quotes in the video, because I was born in the eighties.

95   I spend more time on social media than most of my friends. This used to be because I was depressed and alone, now it's because I don't really have a proper job. "What did you do today, Scott?" someone might ask me if I had a social life, "Oh, I was just working on that 18,000-word essay analysing my own rap songs."

96   Referring, of course, to the song "I'm A Rapper".

97   This is a reference to a video made and uploaded during my first year of university with a man who is now-married and a coffee salesman. It was called "I'm A Prostitute" and is very crude and offensive. Hand me a guitar any time there's no one I want to respect me around, and I'll play it for you, whoever you are. No filming.

98   When the coffee salesman got engaged, he told me to make sure it was removed from the internet. It is, but I still have a copy, though unless either of us become anti-sex-worker politicians, the worst thing its release could ever do is get people singing along to a catchy undergraduate melody. Again, though, lots of what was *acceptable* "humour" back in 2007/8 would not be acceptable now, so maybe the repercussions my friend feared *could* occur.

But that's just a dream, that'll never ever happen,
I can call myself a rapper but that doesn't mean I am one.
I've failed at everything that I've ever fucking tried,[99]
It's not a surprise that my YouTube career has sadly died.

[chorus]:   *I'll never be a YouTube celebrity* [x 8]
                  [as in the previous one, as the refrain repeats there is
                  some "skatting" using the words of the chorus, but this
                  time it becomes increasingly frenzied and physical]

[sung]

I'll never be a YouTube celebriteeeeeeeeee.[100]

99   This is a bleak line, but the kind of statement I would continue to make, and to feel quite
directly, for many years. By now, in 2018, it's *not true*. I've achieved a few things. This shamefully self-
indulgent essay, my dog, my lover, my poems… things that I have made an effort for, and been rewarded
with. My lover is like literally my dream lover, I have properly lucked out there. (Still continues as well in the
Summer of 2020. The isolation of lockdown would, to be blunt, have been catastrophic had I been in my
2014-2017 situation[s].)
100   This final note is held for about fifteen seconds, but is off-key and demonstrates the lo-fi,
imperfect aesthetic. Was this a genuine unwillingness to rerecord the vocal track or a 2013 decision to
embrace my own imperfection, compounded by its inclusion in a song that explores my lack of "success"?
It's an interesting question. Correction: It's an interesting question *for me*.

Video Notes:

Entirely shot "on location" in my teenage bedroom. Though I hadn't lived in it by this point for almost six years, it wasn't redecorated by my parents until years later. This video, oddly, provides an in-depth study of the layout of the room where I lost my virginity, the room where I first read Oscar Wilde, the room where I killed Bowser by swinging him by the tail and throwing him at bombs in *Mario 64*.[101] Visually, this video means more to me than it could ever mean to anyone else. I wasn't happy, spending a night there in 2013 and recording a depressing song about my continual feeling of failure, and nor was I happy much as a teenager. But it's valuable to have, this: do *you* have a visual memory of your lost teenage bedroom???

Performance Notes:

The opening guitar solo is definitely the most accomplished bit of musicianship within Hip-Scott's oeuvre, but the excessive skat/vocal solos and the resultant off-notes (caused by audible vocal strain) make the track distinctly unbeautiful. Is this self-sacrifice? Self-contempt? Elsewhere, the slow melodies and gentle acoustic instrumentation make this the most pleasant of all Hip-Scott to listen to. Also, the rapping is clear, unslurred and an appropriate speed for my abilities. Nice.

Track Rating:

3/5 – flawed, but is it deliberately so? Scott Manley Hadley's Hip-Scott looks at himself, both mockingly and self-effacingly, with self-care but also self-contempt. It's an intriguing concept, but isn't given the mature exploration it deserved/s.

---

101   I also wrote, sang and recorded well over a hundred original songs there. I spent a few weeks trying to write *Lost* (what would now be called) fanfic songs and hoped they'd go viral (did we say viral in 2006?) on MySpace. Even with the couplet, "The monster's coming for you, It killed Mr Eko, it'll kill you too," it failed to take off.

5. The SEX Rap

March 15th, 2013

Lyrics: [102]

A man
And a woman
Alone
In a room. They're gonna get it on.

They're gonna fuck, they're gonna make each other come,
They're gonna sweat, they're gonna kiss, grind and rub,
They're gonna suck each other's nipples, they're gonna grope each other's buns[103],
They're gonna do all the things they know they wanna get done.

But the problem with this modern world of constant sex,
Is that people come not with a fantasy, but with things they expect,
There are a million things to do just between a lover's fucking thighs,
How is anyone ever meant to know the moves that are right?

[chorus]   *I don't know what to do,*
              I don't know what to do,
              I don't know what to do,
              When I'm making love to you.[104]

Let's start with the basics, let's set up the mood,
Are there ideal types of places, ideal pre-sex food?
Whether you're fucking for the first time or the eighty-fucking-third,
You both need to want it, you both need to feel cool.

You both need to be somewhere where you can feel relaxed,
The last thing you want is to be stressed while you shag.
Is it candles? is it oysters? Rose petals? is there a song?
What's the best way for you to feel ready to get it on?

---

102   This is one of the most competent and original of Hip-Scott's songs, and it is pleasing to see a return of my self-confidence so soon after the misery of 'YouTube Celebrity (I'll Never Be A)'. For a long time, this video was officially banned from the internet, as my ex-partner objected to me discussing sex and sexuality in public, as she believed that any mention of sex in my output implied an open discussion of *her* sexual experiences and sex life. I don't believe this is necessarily true, and I feel that the tone and content of 'The SEX Rap' is clearly detached from implied personal experience, and the later verse about being "too repressed to sustain an erection" is obviously hyperbolic and self-satire. I'm repressed, but I'm not *impotent*.
103   "buns" is English slang for arse cheeks, i.e. buttocks. At least, I think it is.
104   The chorus is recorded with both bass and falsetto vocal tracks, as well as the lead vocal, creating the sound of a small choir of Scott Manley Hadleys. Wowza.

Stir a few fucking grams of MDMA
Into a magnum of champagne, drink inhibitions away?[105]
Or form a long-term bond of love and respect,
One where you're comfortable[106] to ask "Can I shit on your chest?"

[repeat chorus]

What gets you wet? What makes you hard?
Such essential questions, so non-normative to ask.
Takes about thirty fucking seconds of your motherfucking time,
To work out, vaguely, what your lover fucking likes.

Do they like lingerie, are they into being slapped?
Do they like being tied up, do they like to fucking dance?
Are they oral, anal, penal or vaginal-led,
Do they prefer the shower or, more classic, the bed?

Do they want to get licked out, do they want to get wanked?
Do they want their thighs bitten, do they want to be spanked?
Do they want their cock rubbed on your pants 'til it burns?
Do they want to hold off nudity until they feel like it's been earned?

Do they want your dick tickling the depths of their mouths?
Do they want your tits against their cheeks, feel them all around?
Do they want a wet clitoris rubbed against their bell-end's hungry tip?
Are they flaunting their anus so you can ram a finger deep in it?

Is her pussy fucking deep? Is his penis fucking thick?
Is it sexy when out tongues meet without connecting in a kiss?
Do you want me to watch you strip, do you like to be undressed?
When I'm sucking you off do you want to grip me by head?

---

105   I've never attended an orgy, but I always imagine this is the cocktail I'd want fuelling me if I
were to do so. Probably Viagra as well – I imagine orgies aren't cheap to attend (especially not with multiple
bags of mandy and magnums of champagne on top of the entrance fee and travel and dog-sitting costs), so it
would probably be sensible to drop a tiny bit more cash to ensure I "got my money's worth". I'm interested
in the social politics of orgies, but – sexually – it's not an idea that excites me, or anyone else I've ever spoken
to about them. I know some couples who are polyamorous, but I've never been able to get an in-depth
conversation about the practicalities of an orgy out of them, because apparently there is a gulf between the
ultra-hetero orgy scene and the far more queer poly scene. I don't particularly want to fuck several people
in the same day (I once had sex with three different women in *the same calendar year* and I haven't stopped
feeling like a [select as appropriate] motherfucking P.I.M.P/disgraceful sinner ever since), but I'd like to *know
about* orgies. Much like I don't want to *receive oral sex from a bear*, but I have read and would read again *Bear*
by Marian Engel. You can read my thoughts on *Bear* at *TriumphOfTheNow.com* (use the search function).
106   This word – I'm transposing many of these lyrics from watching the videos, I never wrote most
of them down – could either be "confident" or "comfortable", but I think "comfortable" makes more sense.

[repeat chorus]

Now, I'm too repressed to ask any of these questions,
I'm almost too repressed to sustain an erection.[107]
It's the curse of being born middle-English, middle-class,
We're culturally conditioned to see all fucking as wrong. [108]

But it's all just madness, doesn't make any sense,
Only the tiniest fraction live a life free of sex,
But it's so weirdly normal to keep it behind closed doors,
Seeing any kind of lust as a character flaw.[109]

But fuck all that, we've had the nineteen-sixties,
We should be proud to say "I love cock", "I love titties"[110]
If someone says, "Shove an avocado up my ass,"
Your only question should be, "Does it have to be a Hass?"[111]

[repeat chorus x 2, with Hip-Scott shouting "and you and you and you
[etc]" after the music ends, pointing at various imaginary lovers]

---

107   Lol I wish. Lol, no, I don't. Sex is actually very enjoyable, it turns out, as long as you're not doing it with someone you fear!

108   For some reason, this couplet loses the (otherwise) ever-present rhyme scheme. Again, if Hip-Scott took more *care* with his rapping, this would not happen.

109   Maybe it was just me who did this, and only in relation to my self-image. In many ways, I still do. I feel a lot of unfulfilled desire.

110   I honestly think the recording session for this song is the only time I have ever said "titties" aloud in my life. It just isn't what people say, is it? Or is it? I don't know, I'm a naïf.

111   In many ways, this entire song was a justification to say this this crass, uber-millennial, couplet.

Video notes:

The video is the least impressive thing about the song, entirely spliced together from two shots, seemingly recorded live as the vocal track was laid down. It's in a kitchen, Hip-Scott has neither a particularly exciting haircut nor outfit: the video is unimpressive.

Performance Notes:

A funky tune, some strong lyrics, but some of the rhymes are lost, and Hip-Scott also seems a little nervous while singing his crude, lewd, words.

Track Rating:

A low 4/5: has the potential to be great, but insignificant effort in both vocal performance and video makes this one of the weaker Hip-Scott tracks that are strong[112].

---

112   For me, that sentence is perfectly clear.

6. Pass The Dostoevsky On The Left Hand Side

May 4th, 2013 *

2013 acoustic demo   heavy drag hop 2015

Lyrics: [113] [114]

I've got a problem that I can't control
I've got a sickness and it is burning me deep into my soul
I've got an addiction, keeping me up every night,
I love it so much, I don't even try to fight.

[chorus]
> *It ain't the cocaine, no, and it ain't the booze,*
> *It ain't the heroin that is giving me the blues,*
> *It ain't the hashish or the speed that has got me hooked,*
> *I'm spending all my mother-fucking money on books.*

When I wake up in the morning, the first thing I do,
Is I ingest a line or two:
Of poetry, man, or motherfucking prose,
It warms me from my head to my toes.

I'm using literature as an emotional crutch,
It's more acceptable than drugs but it costs me as much.
Every time I pass a book store I go in and buy,
It's a compulsion that I struggle to deny.

They see me outside with the cash in my hand,
So desperate for a page I'd even take an Ayn Rand,[115]
Cuz without a book I just can't get by,
So pass the Dostoevsky on the left hand side.[116]

---

113   As indicated by the multiple extant versions of this piece (there is also a 2017 Solid Bald (see below) version which is available at: https://youtu.be/BTMvT8BbVng), this remains an "active" Hip-Scott track. (Note from Summer 2020: I also performed this live at the 2018 launch of *Bad Boy Poet*, which I discuss in reference to 'I'm A Poet' below.)

114   Due to the numerous recorded versions of this song in existence, I have selected the lyrics that seem to resemble the "ideal" performance of the song.

115   There are fewer footnotes here than elsewhere because the quality and the directness of the lyrics improves as Hip-Scott's career develops. There is less to *explain*. However, I should correct this lyric implying that reading Ayn Rand would only be undertaken by a *desperate* person, which obviously isn't true. Ayn Rand is *mostly* read by people who are *desperate* for nothing, but *greedy* for the world. Always remember, though, the end of her life: Rand was a hypocrite and – by her own standards – a *failure*.

116   A reference to "Pass the Duchie on the Left-Hand Side", a song about sharing (yawn) marijuana.

[chorus]

When I say I've got issues you know I don't mean
Of a literary fiction-containing magazine,
I'm talking about the hole in my life
That I fill with print all day and all night.

It's bad for my eyesight and for socialising
To vegetate in a chair with a volume of Dryden.
My life ain't filled with bottles and joints,
I'm all about Woolf, Kerouac and Joyce.

My ideal Friday I'm not wired on speed,
I'm sat in an armchair having a nice quiet read.
I don't lust coke, champagne and MDMA[117],
I want a good Fitzgerald, a great Hemingway.

I want BS Johnson, Sylvia Plath,
Iris Murdoch, not a big bag of crack.
Knausgaard, Allende, early[118] Donna Tartt,
Not a needle full of smack sticking out of my arse[119].

You say "green"[120], I think Graham,
Life's not like *Leaving the Atocha Station*[121]
Books not bongs, hardbacks not wraps,
One gram of powder or the full works of Proust?

I can't be alone this corrupted in life,
So pass the Dostoevsky on the left hand side.
I love to get high off the world of fiction,
I'm a mess, man, I've got a sick addiction.

[repeat chorus]

---

117   That pairing again!
118   In one of the bitchiest acts of my rap oeuvre, all versions of this song dating from after the release
of *The Goldfinch* have the adjective "early" appended to the reference to Donna Tartt's work. Burn!
119   In some versions of the rap this is arm, in others it is arse. Either way, it's not a great couplet.
120   Do people call marijuana "green"? This line makes no sense unless that is true.
121   The 2011 novel by Ben Lerner (rather than the John Ashbery poem it takes its name from),
which contains a LOT of casual drug use.

Video notes:

The earliest version is a simple to-camera performance with an acoustic guitar. The later, "drag-hop" performance is a raunchy, sexed-up, much heavier piece that involves Hip-Scott blowing mounds of flour racked up as if snortable narcotics at the camera. Fishnets, sequins, a little flash of arse-cheek. Powerful stuff.

Performance Notes:

All quite different, but a clear love of the source material, and a very personal connection to the lyrics, makes the selection difficult to critique.

Track Rating:

If I could give higher than 5/5, I would. Actually, I can, can't I? These rules are mine to break. I'm gonna give 'Pass The Dostoevsky On The Left-Hand Side' a solid 6/5. This is the song that has kept me *believing in* Hip-Scott whenever I allow the dream to die. If I can write and rap this piece's finest couplets, I have **potential**. 'Pass the Dostoevsky on the Left Hand Side' makes me love myself, and there isn't much I can say that about.

7. I've Got a Cat

March 15th, 2013*

*   exact date uncertain, but pre-dates the following track as the 'acoustic demo' video trials its green screen technology.

53

Lyrics:

I've got a cat and I motherfucking like it,
I've got a cat, vacuum cleaners frighten it,
I've got a cat, I feed it twice every day,
I've got a cat, I clean its excrement away.

I've got a cat and it's cooler than you,
I've got a cat I bet you wish you did too,
I've got a cat and it's my best friend,
I've got a cat it ain't never gonna end.[122]

---

122   My cat (who probably still lives, alas, but I will never see again) was called Diana, and everything said about her in this song is true. She was, for a period, my *best friend*. She was cool and aloof and scared of vacuum cleaners. But she also didn't get on with Cubby, my dog. And Cubby I paid for, my ex paid for Diana. She wasn't an affectionate cat, but she was pretty, and from time to time she would enjoy attention. She never bonded with Cubby, so it wasn't like I was *tearing a family apart*. I love Cubby, so much. But I do miss Diana. She was fun, if standoffish. (Note from Summer 2020: I spoke about this divvying-up of pets at length in an interview with hip magazine *Vice* last year, available here: https://www.vice.com/en_uk/article/gyzezq/pet-custody-after-breakup-uk?)

Video notes:

Simple, in front of a green screen. Hip-Scott looks happy here, which makes me sad.

Performance Notes:

Both versions are simple. And emotive. Because I do miss my cat.

Track Rating:

1/5 – I'd forgotten how much I missed my cat until I watched this again. For that reason, it's the lowest possible grade.

8. In The Land of the Dinosaurs

October 8th, 2013

An introductory note is required here, because rather than a straightforward "song" with an accompanying video, 'In The Land Of The Dinosaurs' is in fact a cohesive short film, structured as if a live-action video. Making heavy use of amateur green-screen technology, it features Hip-Scott jumping through a black hole back in time to "the land of the dinosaurs", where – after being chased by a velociraptor, he meets another time-travelling version of himself. There is no visual or auditory attempt to differentiate the two versions of Hip-Scott, which in hindsight is an error. The following is the pre-rap dialogue:

Hip-Scott A: Me?

Hip-Scott B: Oh yes, me!

Hip-Scott A: But what am I doing here?

Hip-Scott B: I'm you from the future, and I've come here to seduce ya.

Hip-Scott A: To seduce me?

Hip-Scott B: I'm from the future: for me, it's already happened.

Lyrics: [123]

I'm one goddamn sexy motherfucker,
Every time I see a mirror I just think "I wanna be my lover"[124],
And now it's time to take that chance,
It's every man's dream to fuck himself up the ass.[125]

I've got a unique opportunity,
Making love to myself, I know the ways to please me,
Why the hell would I say "no"?
Making love to myself, never ever gonna take it too slow.[126]

Umm ummm[127] gonna get it on with myself,
Umm ummm gonna teach my dick what pleasure can be all about.
Gonna make myself come so hard
When I fuck myself right up the motherfucking arse.

I've travelled back in time to turn me on,
I've travelled back in time so that I can get it on
I'm gonna [indecipherable][128] pull out my dick,
Teach myself what to do with it.

---

123   Given the overall sloppiness of the video, I have gently edited these lyrics so that they make sense. The use of singular and plural first person alternates in the video, however I think a consistent "I" is preferable.

124   There have been periods of my life where I have been (or, have felt like I have been) very good-looking. Right now is not one of those times: I am typing this at the fattest I have ever been. I need to get back into the habit of cycling everywhere, all the time. And cut down on the cava, get back on the gin. (Note from Summer 2020: this situation improved slightly, but then with the closing down of life in Spring 2020 I again put on weight. I'm in a little better shape again now, but I still find myself fucking repulsive. Still thinner than I was in Barna, tho, lol.)

125   I don't think this is "every man's dream", it certainly isn't mine. I've never really understood the appeal of anal sex. Tbf, I've only ever tried it when wasted, and on no occasion was it my idea or suggestion and I found it quite uncomfortable. Though, as I mentioned above, my penis is relatively thick, so maybe my loss is the less-girthy gentleman's gain?

126   If fucking yourself, Hip-Scott argues, you could skip foreplay. What if, though, sex with the self is like tickling – i.e. it doesn't work? My thesis is that this is unlikely, because masturbation works alone, but until this exact scenario is tested by the sex-scientists of the future, we cannot be certain.

127   These are delivered basically as grunts, the kind of noise one might make while sexually thrusting.

128   Possibly this is meant to be "take off my jeans", but in his excitement my younger self lost the ability to enunciate.

60

Engaging with my own sexuality
By literally having sex with me.
Gonna fool around, gonna bust some moves,
Don't worry 'bout pain, I've brought plenty of lube.[129]

[sung]

In the land of the dinosaurs you can travel back in time and make love to
yourself
In the land of the dinosaurs you can travel back in time and make love
make love make a lotta love lotta love lotta lotta love to yourself
Make a lotta love make a lotta lotta lotta love
You can travel back in time and make-a love to yourself
Make love, make a lotta love to yourself
In the land of the dinosaurs you can travel back in time and make a lotta
love to yourself
In the land of the dinosaurs you can travel back in time and make a lotta
love to yourself
To yourself, to yourself, to yourself oh yeah
To yourself, to yourself, to yourself oh yeah
In the land of the dinosaurs you can travel back in time and make a lotta
love to yourself
Self self
To yourself, self, self.[130]

[spoken] Probably shouldn't tell anybody about that.[131]

---

129   Every occasion – to date – on which I inserted my slightly larger than average penis into another
human's anal cavity, it was quite a painful experience. I've never had anything larger or longer than a finger
up my own anus, so I have no idea how spacious it would be. I doubt I'd enjoy fucking myself up the arse,
to be honest. This whole song is a crude joke.
130   Too many of these songs include long-winded and untuneful skats/vocal solos. This one I
bothered to transcribe because – as a crude, immature man – this is one of my favourites of my own raps.
131   Teehee.

Video notes:

The shit use of green screen technology makes for a crude, but self-consciously so, experience. It's fun for me to watch.

Performance Notes:

Solid, sexy, clear; dancing like a cute little time traveller. Hip-Scott *was* hot shit.

Track Rating:

It's gotta be a full 5/5[132] for this one. In my opinion, the beat is funky, the lyrics are witty and it's a real treat to see my younger self in triplicate at the end of the song, with so much hair, so beautiful. This video is *exactly* my style of humour. I often sing it to myself, and have done for years. I am, truly, *proud* of 'In The Land of the Dinosaurs', and if I ever gain the courage to rap live, this would *definitely* make the set. Joyful.[133]

---

132   Of course, this is rating it 5/5 in comparison to the quality of other Hip-Scott tracks. I'm not saying this is a perfect mini-musical in comparison to *proper real life musicals*, I'm saying it is a *perfect* Hip-Scott video. It's got a catchy tune and some lovely gags.

133   (From Summer 2020: I did perform 'In The Land of the Dinosaurs' live at the 2018 launch of *Bad Boy Poet*, where it got a lot of laughs, positioned as it was after I read a very heavy piece about my parents' dual degenerative diseases, titled 'I wish I could watch Dante's Peak every night'. I got confused/shy in the middle, though, and skipped two verses.)

9. Born to Rap

December 5th, 2013

Lyrics: [134]

[spoken] Hello. Good evening, good afternoon. A lot of people have accused me of not taking my responsibilities to the world of hip-hop seriously. But let's pay some reparations on my soul.

[toasts the camera, begins rapping]

It's been a few months since I last did a rap[135],
But watch out motherfuckers Hip-Scott is back,
I'm here to drop beats and I'm here to spit verse,
The good boy[136] of hip-hop don't ride in no hearse.[137]

I've been writing away[138], biding my time,
Licking my lips before they spit sweet rhyme.
If you're ready, motherfuckers, I will give it to you,
Because rapping is what I was born to do.

Some people born to rap, some people born to die,
Some people born to succeed, some people born to get high,
Some people born to hate, some people born to kill,
Some of us born with lyrical skill.

---

134   I had completely forgotten this rap song existed. I was busy at the time, studying a lot, working a lot, writing a lot and socialising a lot. And still I managed to keep rapping. This is, without a doubt, the weakest of *all the raps included here*. Remember those Uniqlo jeans, though, one of the best pairs of trousers I ever had.

135   According to my stats here, less than two.

136   While, perhaps, the antics of some "gangster rappers" is actively criminal, I can hardly be described as a "good boy". I have done many things that are immoral, and my debut poetry collection is titled *Bad Boy Poet*, showing that – with age – I know myself better than I did then. Also, the video for this song and the new-found nasality to the voice demonstrate that the Hip-Scott of late 2013 was not the best behaved Hip-Scott of all... (Note from Summer 2020: When I first submitted that debut collection, the title was presented like this: *[Bad] [Boy] [Poet]*, which was intentional as it was able to evoke several different meanings that were lost with the deletion of the square brackets. Though the text deals with – in my own words of the time – "contemporary masculinities", it was written before I'd started identifying – to myself and myself only – as non-binary. I wasn't good at being a "boy", I wasn't good at being a "male" figure, and I wanted to question that more directly. I have been doing so, this year, in poems that no one wants to publish. An email rejection came through for a submission of a couple of them while I was typing this paragraph lol. See Appendix A. (It was the "serious limerick" that just got rejected.))

137   I have never ridden in a hearse, still. Only ever been to two funerals. (Note from Summer 2020: I attended a third funeral during my first Summer in Canada, as my lover's plus-one. It was the funeral of her grandmother, who I never met. I also didn't ride in the hearse. It was in Ottawa, a surprisingly beautiful city!)

138   Yeah, but not hip-hop.

Cuz my rapping talent, it is undisputed[139],
Rhymes so shocking I feel electrocuted.
When Destiny speaks, she spits into a mic,
It's motherfucking fate, it can't be denied.

[chorus][140]
>*Born to rap,*
>*Born to rap, motherfucker,*
>*Born to rap,*
>*Born to rap, motherfucker.*

Look at the heavens, read the stars,
Hip-Scott is shining down on you, wherever you are.[141]
Verse elevated, on an astral plane,
Hip-hop will never be the same again.[142]

When I come, I jizz rhyme, when I'm cut, I bleed verse[143],
I said [indecipherable], I got a physical curse,
My lyrics are my tongue, sweet like Toblerone[144],
If my rap was your lover, you'd wanna get it alone.

Frottage[145] for the ears, twerking for the soul,
Lyrics say nothing but they make you feel whole.[146]
My hip-hop is a vehicle and I've got the key,
Jump in the backseat, rap is coming with me.

---

139   True, in that no one disputes its non-existence.
140   The chorus is out of tune and genuinely quite difficult to listen through, even though it's only ten seconds long.
141   Like Mufasa in *The Lion King*.
142   In the least self-effacing way possible, I think it's accurate to say that in no way did Hip-Scott influence hip-hop.
143   Lies: semen and blood, respectively.
144   You what, mate???
145   Rubbing off genitals through clothing. It's a word I use a lot. Often erroneously referred to as "dry humping", an utterly inappropriate term because an act of frottage in which all participants remain dry *has failed as frottage*.
146   None of the lyrics written and performed by Hip-Scott make *even me* "feel whole", and I doubt they're inspirational for anyone else either.

Wasn't born in the ghetto, never lived on the streets[147],

147   I spent a period of 2017 *technically* homeless. I won't go into it here, but it was both humbling and inspiring and there is more on this in the finale piece of *Bad Boy Poet* (Open Pen, 2018). Which is (thankfully) better than these rap lyrics, all of them. (Note from Summer 2020: So, right, actually, I will go into it here. What happened was this: when my relationship with my ex ended, my self-confidence and self-belief was at such a low ebb, I genuinely didn't believe I would be able to reintegrate with society again. I had lived in houses owned by my lover and her family since I left university, and I had been in and out of work as and when I was "able" to do so. I didn't think I'd be able to work consistently and pay rent, I didn't think I'd be able to date, I didn't think I'd be able to take care of myself and I didn't think any of these factors would ever change. This fear translated into me, terrified of never having any stability, taking out a massive bank loan very rashly and using it, along with the tiny, empty gesture "severance package" my ex gave me, to buy a narrowboat in Leicestershire which I planned to sail (is that the right verb?) down to London and live on, as you are allowed to park up on the canal banks for two weeks at a time, as long as you then move ~1km. I'm a bit hippieish, and I kept meeting weird people who were living the mobile boat life at events in East London, though, most of them started with more money than I did. I paid a four figure sum for a survey on the second boat I found within my budget (called 'Pegasus'), which it passed with the caveat that there were a couple of minor welding jobs that needed to be done. While waiting for my appointment in the dry dock to get the work done, my carpenter grandfather and I spent a couple of days repanelling the walls, which I then painted. I bought a composting toilet and lots of other useful things, was on the cusp of buying extra solar panels and a low energy fridge, with the plan to move onto it and get it down to London in late September 2017, after the engineers at the boatyard where I'd bought it had completed the small repairs. When the boat was removed from the water again (the first time had been for the formal inspection, the survey), the boatyard "discovered" major structural damage, which would have required the entire hull (that's the bottom) of the boat to be replaced, at a cost basically the same as the entire fucking boat. In theory, as the surveyor had missed this issue *and verbally acknowledged culpability in a phone call I foolishly didn't record*, he should have paid for it, and all would have been well. He refused, though, and then decided to communicate with me only via his insurance provider, who completely ignored my formal, written, appeal which left me with three options: 1) try to independently pursue a settlement through small claims court, 2) hire a lawyer and formally sue the surveyor and/or his insurer, or 3) walk away, sell the boat back to the boatyard "for scrap" and get on with my life. To be honest, I think I was conned, and the boatyard and the surveyor were likely in cahoots (he had been the "only available" surveyor from the list of six "real names" they provided me with), knowing that I was a bratty Londoner with money in the bank (how were they to know it was almost entirely a loan?) who could easily be strung along for a bit of cash, and likely intimidated by pursuing legal proceedings. If this was what they thought, they were right. For several months, though, they kept gradually raising prices of possible repairs and making promises about completion dates, and I travelled to London every weekend to work and back to my parents' where I could easily drive (or be driven) to the boatyard and continue working on the boat. I slept on friends' sofas and floors and spare rooms and beds (thank you, thank you, thank you to David Bamford, Sean Preston & his wife Helen, Joe Hancock & Jess Banting, Edie Culshaw & Joe von Malachowski, Arianne Clarke & her posh housemates who didn't like me, the ephemeral Frank DuBois and also to [name redacted], a woman I met on a dating app who had no qualms with having a brief fling with a bald, technically homeless, masculinised individual) and my mental health continued to decline as I felt a lot of pressure to hire a lawyer (as the "mature" response) but felt terrified by the risk of *further* financial losses. I also had no home, which is tough. I remember cycling back to David Bamford's one night, from a shift working a party in Loughborough Junction, when I had to pull over by the railings in front of a church just north of Camberwell Green to have a panic attack so severe that I called an ambulance on myself because I didn't feel I could get up and move ever again. I was suicidal. I was on Valium for a week, which – I have to say – is the best intoxicant I've ever consumed, and I totally wasted the ones I had left while attending a boozy family event with my lover's family in Toronto, when the lovely Valium got lost among sloshing wine. So, yes, by December 2017 and my decision to walk away from the boat and from litigation, I'd lost about ten thousand pounds, which I have attempted to pay back as fast as possible, basically by working almost constantly since Summer 2019. Hopefully, one day, I'll have enough money in my bank account to close the loan and spend more time having fun and/or sleeping, but the debt drags me down, and the fatigue from all the insanely long hours I keep are ageing me faster than I've ever aged before. I'm tired and I'm bored. I'm also barely writing. And every day I'm looking at the package with the dress in that I'm not wearing, even though I want to be wearing my dress more than I want to do just about anything else in the world. Did this footnote make sense?)

There ain't nothing grimey about my motherfucking beats.
I'm spitting no lies, making no false claim,
I was created as Hip-Scott, it is my name.[148]

[repeat chorus]

If everyone could motherfucking spit like me,
The world would be a much more hip-hop place to be.
Dancing in the street like Jagger and Bowie[149],
A Rapper's Delight, don't know who that's by, sorry.[150]

But the point remains, hip-hop sets you free,
Which is something all of us need to aspire to be.
Throw off your clothes, rap naked in the sky,[151]
Write your best fucking lyrics on your inside thigh.[152]

Words and music, music or words,
They're immediate art forms that need to be heard.
Now this isn't poetry, this isn't shit[153],
It's lo-fi hip-hop that isn't taking the piss.[154]

---

148   This line contains both lies and false claims.

149   Racistly, both Google (in September 2018 in Catalunya) and my younger self think of the inferior 1980s Mick Jagger and David Bowie version of the Motown classic first. It *should say* Martha and the Vandellas. Did you know it was co-written by Marvin Gaye? I didn't, until September 2018.

150   I do, it's the Sugarhill Gang, and tbh I'm disgusted at my younger self for even joking about not knowing that. More lies/false claims.

151   If you did a parachute jump with no clothes on, would the backpack with the parachute in *technically* stop you from being naked?

152   Not certain what I meant by this, I think I was just trying to be bawdy. There's a lot of sexual frustration in these raps. A prurience that in no way matched my life.

153   This isn't poetry, but it is shit.

154   And I suppose it is this line that sums up the confusing way I still feel about this project, i.e. 'Hip-Scott' as a whole: I don't think it *was* "taking the piss", at least not simplistically. But if it wasn't, what *was* it for? *Who* was it for? Why did I think it was a sensible activity to pour time into? Why am I still looking at it now, years on? Is anyone even reading this footnote? Are you even real??? (Have I really continued editing and revising this text for TWO YEARS???)

Just cuz I'm white and taking a fucking degree,
Doesn't mean that hip-hop should be closed off to me,
I'm using this genre with a bit of respect,
There's nothing condescending about my trying to spit.[155]

[repeat chorus]

---

155   This last verse feels a bit forced, y'know, like I kinda understood that my class and ethnicity rendered my interest in hip-hop somewhat suspect. I don't claim to have any rights to the genre, but nor am I 100% comfortable (in the more progressive 2018) in saying that what I'm trying to express isn't often as culturally insensitive as the manner in which I'm expressing them, i.e. the lyrics in the first rap equating infidelity with domestic violence. There are troubling sentiments in some of these rashly made raps.

Video notes:

As with some of the earlier pieces, it's just shots of Hip-Scott around the house. Some feather boas and toilet shots can't save this.

Performance Notes:

Musically uninteresting, lots of lyrics lost due to poor delivery. An absolute shambles.

Track Rating:

1/5: There's not much to like here. The rapping isn't high quality, and though there are some fun shots in the video filmed by sellotaping my phone to the kitchen ceiling, *I forgot this existed*, which is as damning a review as a Hip-Scott track can have.

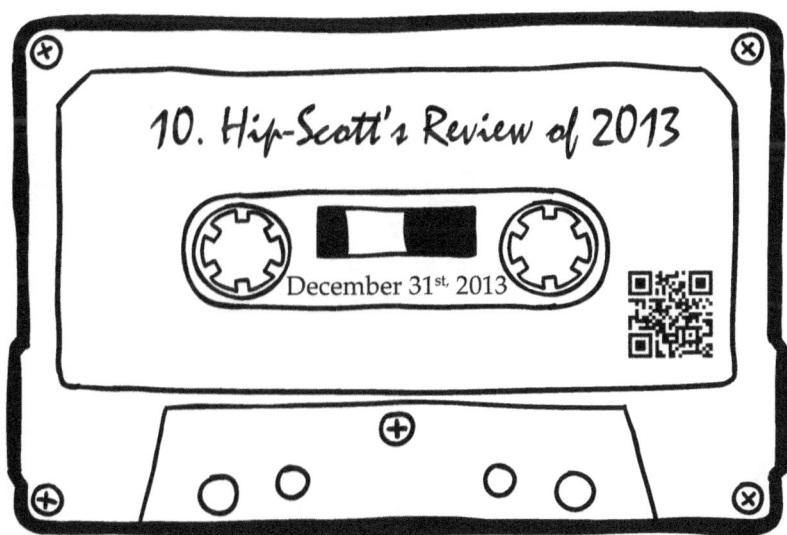

10. Hip-Scott's Review of 2013

December 31st 2013

Lyrics: [156]

Welcome to Hip-Scott's review of 2013,
The year that's now over, a year that has been
Different to those before it, different to those still to come,
A year where I've probably had a little bit too much fun.[157]

Regressing, medicating[158], writing and jazz[159],
Some unexpected experiences, but few of them bad.
Shitloads of parties, and being back behind a bar,
Getting out of Europe and travelling reasonably far.[160]

Improving my Spanish, developing my rap,
Reading big fucking books, using a full rucksack.
Quitting office job, returning to school,
Accidentally behaving like I was trying to be cool.[161]

[sings (badly) some lines from Macklemore & Ryan Lewis' 'Thrift Shop']

I saw a lot of places I had never been before,
Went to Venice[162], Rome, Stonehenge and more,
Andalucía in Spain and across to Tangier,
Chefchaouen, Fez, Marrakesh, the desert.

Read *Ulysses* in a binge of literary pretence[163]
Sat in Essaouira on the old sea defence.[164]
Idyllic days of joy sat next to the waves,
The Atlantic ahead [indecipherable] shimmering haze.

---

156   Maybe when I did this I intended to make it an annual event. There has never been another Hip-Scott review of a year.

157   i.e. socialising and intoxication.

158   Both self-medicating with intoxicants and taking anti-depressants.

159   I listened to *a lot* of jazz back then. Hooooeeeeee, good times! I love bebop.

160   For more detailed descriptions of my 2013 trip backpacking around Southern Europe and North Africa, head to the tag "med-hopping" on my blog: www.triumphofthenow.com/tag/med-hopping/

161   i.e. socialising and intoxication.

162   I have only been to Venice once in my life, and it was in early 2013 when I was horrendously depressed. I found being in Venice deeply troubling, because I walked through its gorgeous streets, strolled through St Mark's Square and was *surrounded* by beauty and it made no difference to my mood, no difference at all. I remember I was stood in front of the Doge's Palace and I started weeping because I was **in fucking Venice**, and I still just wanted to be erased from existence. What this rap doesn't mention is the two lazy suicide attempts I made in the Spring. I wanted to be dead, but I was scared of the **process of dying**, so I didn't consume enough of what I took to try and overdose.

163   It *is* inherently pretentious to read *Ulysses*.

164   Which is used as a shooting location in *Game of Thrones*, though I didn't watch *Game of Thrones* until 2014 so have no photos of me pretending to be in the show.

Through the Atlas mountains [indecipherable]
Infinite Jest [indecipherable]
[indecipherable] Tunisia, Palermo,
Missing a train, taking two internal flights to make good.[165]

Greece, some islands, a little bit of driving,
Then back to England to try to engage with
My life as an adult in the country that I'm from,
Tail between my legs, struggling to get on.

[sings (badly) the chorus hook from Daft Punk (feat Pharell)'s 'Get Lucky']

2013 was a bad year for music,
With inexcusable misogyny excused by funkiness[166].
But I don't engage with contemporary culture,
So here's a little verse about some books that I've read.

I discovered a writer who is fucking amazing,
His name is Malcolm Lowry, he wrote *Under the Volcano.*
All his books are about depression and booze,
Two of my favourite topics (that's some unsurprising news).

I also read *Infinite Jest* and *The Savage Detectives*
Both brilliant, big, well-constructed texts.
I grew into reading poetry for fun,
Which made me feel like an intellectual man.[167]

2013 was elsewhere pretty eventful,
Other than reading and trips off Shit Island.[168]
Of course, I started a postgraduate degree,
Bonded deep with my cat, though she hasn't bonded back with me.[169]

---

165   This is the most decadent thing I have ever done in my life. I had to get from Palermo (in Sicily) to Brindisi (on Italy's Adriatic coast), as I was getting a ferry from there to Greece. I missed the train I needed to take and so flew there via Milan. I have tasted glamour and it is STUPID. I am much happier now that I have a much smaller disposable income. (Note from Summer 2020: worries about the debt I was already in two years ago have continued to grow, exacerbated by the troubling economic turbulence of trying to work through a global pandemic.)

166   Referring to the hit pop song by Robin Thicke, 'Blurred Lines'.

167   I wouldn't start writing poetry in earnest for a while. Is poetry intellectual? No, not the kind I write, at least. (See *Bad Boy Poet* (Open Pen, 2018).)

168   Even before the Brexit referendum, I was referring to England as "Shit Island".

169   While writing the footnotes to 'I've Got A Cat' I became quite emotional. Might have had something to do with the cava I was drinking, it was probably out of date or something.

Learnt a lot about the motherfucking *Bible*,
From a literary perspective,[170] I haven't become a deluded arsehole.[171]
I suppose I developed as a fucking human being,
Learnt better how to be happy, if that's what you wanna hear.[172]

[spoken]

So I suppose it's wise to take a moment to reflect[173] on the mistakes that I've made: it hasn't all been success.

2013 was mixed, some bad things went down.
Diseases and death and vomiting all over town.[174]
I was sad and I was angry, but the things that will stay in my memory are the good moments, these are the things that cannot be taken away.[175]

Thoughts, and the experiences that have made me smile, are the important ones.
The buildings, people, mountains, volcanoes, seas, monuments, ruins, islands, books, museums, foods, drinks, I have seen this year that I will keep close to my heart are those that mattered, those that were new.

And I resolve to see more, experience more, learn more and know more in the year to come.[176]

Because there aren't many left.

---

170   I began writing a sexed-up Biblical philosophical novel in 2013. A few extracts have been published online over the years, but most of it remains private. It was my attempt to write a book with mass market appeal, so it ended up being a jumble of sexualised hyperviolence, cod-philosophy and lots of pooing. Needless to say, it didn't get picked up by a publisher, major or otherwise. It's still available, though, if you or a connection of yours could get good bunse for it??? (See Appendix C.)
171   Quite shockingly anti-religion. Tactless.
172   Learnt "better", yes, but didn't do anything about it for a long time. One of the biggest mistakes of my life was, probably in 2015 or 16, telling my ex-partner that every therapist I had ever had (which is several) told me I should break up with her, or at best make *significant* changes to the way our relationship functioned. I was unhappy in that relationship for many reasons, but a big part of that was time spent amongst people who had diametrically opposed *ideals* to me.
173   The reflection in this piece is very limited and quite impersonal. For more accurate discussion of my thoughts and feelings, check out my blog!
174   Socialising and intoxication.
175   The music behind this section is very mournful, and does *not* give the impression of a man who is hopeful.
176   I didn't experience much more for a while. I just got more sad, more stressed and bald.

There aren't many left.[177]

[sings, badly, but with a clear melancholy, the chorus to Miley Cyrus' 'Wrecking Ball'. When the music stops there is a momentary pause, then the screen cuts to a nude Hip-Scott straddling a red bean bag, singing one line from the chorus of Cyrus' hit.]

---

177   Depression, as I said. I was very depressed. I was convinced that I would be dead soon, I believed it with a wild intensity, but felt like that was a *positive* thing. I didn't want to be alive any more. I dreamed of death. I wanted it I wanted it I wanted it and for years afterwards I hated myself for never quite having had the self-belief to hang myself.

Video notes:

A combination of while-recording shots, and images from the trips and experiences that the lyrics refer to. Feels rushed, and I remember that it was.

Performance Notes:

The mournful spoken word section at the track's end has the potential to be quite powerful, but it never achieves its aims elsewhere. Bad delivery.

Track Rating:

2/5 – Two very weak raps in a row. Lots of mumbling and slurring and very bad singing, but this track is rescued by some pleasing shots from my 2013 backpacking trip, as well as the final two seconds of nude singing. Tbh if those two seconds were a Hip-Scott video by themselves, it would get the full 5/5.

11. XXXMas Special 1 -
Santa, Baby

December 24th 2014*

---

*   Basically a full year between raps here. I spent a lot of time working on the previously-mentioned Biblical novel, and too much time "working on" socialising and intoxication. I also worked quite a lot, too. And my grandmother died of cancer, which I've explored a little in my writing elsewhere (see Appendix D).

Lyrics:

[first verse and chorus of 'Santa, Baby' performed as standard]

Santa Baby, there's a lot of things that I need,
And in exchange for them I am willing to please.
I'm not a tease[178], I am materially-minded,
For a dog I'd wank you off until I was blinded.[179]

I'll sit on your lap, I'll play with your beard,
You can do whatever you want, even if it's weird[180].
There's nothing I wouldn't do for a gift or two,
Everyone has a price and mine is reduced for you.

Santa, Baby, there is a lot that I want,
And I'm willing to pay, but I don't have the dosh.
Top of the list's a puppy, please
It's impractical, yes, but you can't help your dreams!

Fix it up, yeah, and be my middle man
And I'd reward you, of course, with all that I am[181],
Other than a dog, I'd also like a coat[182]
Or flights somewhere outside of Europe.[183]

[repeat chorus of 'Santa, Baby']

---

178   The thing, though, is that I very much *have been* a tease, due to my erotophobia, rather than a prudishness or a lack of lust. I would make people think I wanted to fuck them (and I would want to fuck them) but then I'd run away before I had to. It's funny ("funny weird" rather than "funny haha"), looking back. One of my therapists once suggested I try to engage with my sexuality, but at the time I was like "well what the hell is the point in that when I'm in a long-term sexless relationship", and I stand by that. To learn about your sexual self you need to have a space free of sexual jealousy, and for most – not all – people that can only be found when single.

179   I saved money from working and – just over a year later – bought myself Cubby, my gorgeous perfect dog. He is part of my soul, now, and I love him.

180   What do YOU think Ol' Saint Nick, Father Christmas, Santa Claus, might want to do, sexually, that counts as "weird"?

181   Maybe this should be "all that I can".

182   Pretty certain that until recording this was going to be "some coke".

183   Mispronounced so as to rhyme with "coat".

Video notes:

Hip-Scott in drag and thick lipstick prancing around in front of the camera. What's not to like? For some non-discerning viewers, "Hip-Scott in drag and thick lipstick prancing around in front of the camera".

Performance Notes:

Incredibly crisp and clear vocal delivery, every word can be heard. This boasts probably the closest match between intention and final product.

Track Rating:

A high 4/5. A very sexualised young – and not yet bald – Scott Manley Hadley dances provocatively and promises to exchange sexual favours for gifts.[184] It's a novelty Christmas performance that is on-brand and gently erotic. Doesn't get the full 5/5 because the melody is unoriginal. Actually, fuck it, let's give it the full 5/5, I could do with the ego boost, remembering how depressed I was is making me sad.

---

184   Kinda what I did in real life, actually. The joke was on me, I suppose, and *nobody* had the last laugh.

12. En Toure*

October 17th, 2016**

---

*   This is – knowingly – incorrect French.

**   Other than the November 2015 drag-hop version of 'Pass The Dostoevsky on the Left Hand Side', this is the first appearance of Hip-Scott in a while, and it would be the last time I would place that moniker in the title of a video. The following track, 'XXXMas Special 2 – All I Want For Xmas Is A Wig Made Of My Own Pubes' is what I now consider – tonally, aesthetically – the "last" Hip-Scott song.

Transcript:[185]

How should a rapper be?[186]

At the age of 27[187], Zelda Fitzgerald decided she wanted to be a ballerina. So, what Zelda Fitzgerald did was spend every single free minute she had trying to be a ballerina. She got an offer to be a professional ballerina and and and turned it down. And this obsession – and this rejection she made – ultimately led to her being committed and incarcerated in psychiatric wards until her death by fire.[188]

[the older, stockier, balder, Hip-Scott now performs the first few lines of his very first rap[189]]

They say shit floats, and there ain't nothing shitter hotter hot shitter shit hot more shit than Hip-Scott.
Shitter-hot, hot shit.
They say shit floats, and boy am I shit hot.
They say shit floats, and Hip-Scott is shiiiit.
They say shit floats, and what's shitter than Hip-Scott, what's more hot shit than hip-
They say shit floats, and what's more shit
They say shit floats, and what's more shit than Hip-Scott
Shit hot, hot shit rap
I'm hot

---

185 The majority of this "track" is spoken word, a "skit" track, if you will. However, far from being an attempt at comedy, this video almost performs its own analysis of Hip-Scott. It questions the project and my inconsistent commitment to it.

186 The eternal question, one that still remains unanswered.

187 This video was filmed in the Summer before my 28th birthday, when I too was 27 and unfulfilled, but aware that my ability to die young was soon about to be over. (Note from Summer 2020: I still wish, deep down, that I'd had the nerve to kill myself when I had the urge. I don't hate my current life enough to attempt suicide, but not being alive at all would be better. I suppose, actually, that means I do hate my life. I don't have any friends here in Toronto, I live entirely in my own head. I have a beautiful, wonderful, lover, it is true, and I have Cubby and I've had [very] mild success with the writing I've done, but there's no forward trajectory any more, I'm lonely and, to be completely frank, I'm increasingly and distractingly horny. I want to touch and be touched. I want to dress in clothes that make me feel *sexy* and I want the validation of arousing someone for the first time, of being wanted and being seduced and being accepted as the person I am. My lover makes me feel that, yes, but she is away for an extended period at the moment, working the wine harvest down by the American border, and I daren't leave the house after dark in case I put myself in a situation where I'd allow myself to be led astray. I want to taste a stranger's tongue. I want to taste a stranger's c- "I lack / Anecdotes of death and illicit sex / Not because / I'm a fucking saint / But because / I'm a fucking coward.")

188 I think about Zelda Fitzgerald a lot. I used to feel very much like the Fitzgeralds in my former long term relationship. I was Zelda. Actually, we were both Zelda. Scott Fitzgerald was *successful* and depressed and alcoholic.

189 The physical change since these lyrics' initial pronouncement is conspicuous. There is even some accidental facial hair here, which looks *bad.*

They say shit hot
They say shit floats
And I'm hot shit
Shit shit floats if shit floats then Hip-Scott is
They say shit float
They say[190]

Agéd rapper, Scott Manley Hadley, Hip-Scott…

[raps]

They say hip-hop's dead, but Hip-Scott's alive,
I'm here rapping to you live from a mountainside,
Don't know how to get down, I'm kinda trapped up here,[191]
And what I'm doing is tryna distract myself from the fear
That I'm feelin' inside cuz it's real fuckin' empty,
There's no one around, there's no one to save me,
What I gotta do is get down this cliff,
And I don't have the skills and I don't have the gift,
To climb down rock, cuz I never done it before
I don't know why I climbed up, it was stupid or…

[spoken]

What I need to do is learn how to freestyle.[192]

When I was climbing up here, I was thinking "ooh, climbing, mountain climbing's great, I should do this all the time".
Going down, it's shit. Like, it hurts, it's dangerous, it's quite scary. I keep worrying if there are snakes here. It's not very hip-hop to be scared of snakes, is it?

[raps]

---

190   I really really really really really felt that there was a gag in the use of the slang terms "shit hot", "hot shit", "hot" and "shit". It turns out there wasn't. In the video, these lines are rapidly cut up, with the words displayed on screen, using (I imagine) every single "title animation" available in the free video editing app, iMovie.

191   Visiting Marseille with my unwell father (the second of our three holidays together), I clambered up a mountain in the Calanques National Park. I reached the peak within about ten minutes of goat-like scrabbling across sharp, volcanic, rock, and then spent almost an hour clambering down. The three shots that are used to make 'En Toure' were each filmed as I "rested" on my descent. I would sit down, set up the camera, talk and/or rap at it until I ran out of thought, then move on. I was worried I'd become stuck. I didn't. (Note from Summer 2020: The trip to Amsterdam that one of the pieces in *Bad Boy Poet* is about happened less than a year after this, and the decline of my father in that brief period is the reason why I was so affected by his lost mobility in the Dutch capital. See: https://youtu.be/wbfNaGwdLX8)

192   The freestyling in this video is – for the most part – better than I would have expected of myself.

Fuck that phobia, I ain't scared of snakes,
For me, they just what they represent,
Which is penises, yeah, and they ain't fucking scary,
I'm a man, yeah, ain't got no penis envy.[193]

[raps]

I like to be in the middle of a town,
With a book in my hand and a…
And a…
Book in my bag… that's brown…

[spoken]

I don't know what the accent is that I'm doing, cuz it's different from the one I was doing over there?[194]

Does it need to rhyme?

[raps a couplet from 'Fuck the Police' by N.W.A.[195]]

193   Again, this line oozes a pre-contemporary social consciousness. We now accept that not everyone who is a man has a penis, much as we accept that not everyone who is a woman does not. I'm not being facetious, I am pro-trans rights. (Note from Summer 2020: I refer to myself as a "masculinised person" where previously I would have referred to myself as a "man" and I feel a lot better doing this, but I do also feel nervous that no one has given me permission to do this and because I look like "a man", I feel like describing myself as "non-binary" feels inauthentic. It feels right, but if I don't *need* to tell people, does it count? I'm very fucking conflicted about this, but I feel much more comfortable exploring it in private (or in some writing that very few (if any!) people (hello?) will ever read) than I do discussing it with my friends or family. I also don't want to lose my lover, who I love. My closest trans friend (as in "my closest friend who is trans", rather than "my closest friend, who is trans") lost a long term relationship because his partner resented the transition and I don't want that to happen to me. I should really be speaking to someone professionally about this, I suppose, but silence is easier haha lol whoops.)
194   Some of the freestyle raps in this "doc" are performed with a slight American accent, some have a gentle attempt at a London accent, like you'd hear in grime, which was moving into the mainstream around this time. It's strange, Hip-Scott before was always natural: I'd clearly forgotten my message and forgotten my voice.
195   When I was an undergraduate, I remember at a Welsh open mic night performing, a capella, the first verse of this song. This was like 2008, and I was naïve, so I definitely would have said the "n" word. That is not acceptable and I apologise on behalf of my younger self. Is it unforgiveable, even with this contrition? I hope not, but maybe it is. I now know that it is **wrong** and, even when alone, I refrain from rapping along to hip-hop, as it is important I do not lose sight of the significance of this word and how unwelcome and inappropriate it is, at all times, coming from a white person's mouth. When I first understood the seriousness of this issue (after reading an in-depth interview with Kendrick Lamar), I trained myself to say my dog's name as a substitute when singing along to rap, because the syllable count is the same and I love my dog so thus revel in any and all opportunities to think about him. This, I realised, is also problematic (i.e. stupid and insensitive), so I just stopped singing along to rap music. The loss to me is *far less significant* than the potential offence and hurt that could have been caused had I continued going through life thinking the context of karaoke removed the context of extreme and historic racism. Maybe the admissions in this footnote are the most regrettable content of this entire text. Christ, I really didn't think this would end up being such a long exploration of my own quasi-fictional rap career. This is what, page 87? I'm still here if you are, reader!

Yes, that rhymed.

Y'know, I know nothing about hip-hop.

[This line is like half-sung?]

Jesus was a gangster, he a prankster, yeah, he a gangster, yeah.[196]

[spoken]

You could maybe achieve your dreams, even if those dreams are dreams you only decide are your dreams aged 27 when you should really be grown up and shit.[197]

[screen displays "Hip-Scott will return"[198]]

[spoken]

I think I'm gonna die here.

---

196   No idea what this freestyle was aiming to become or to be. It's shit. I'm glad it wasn't developed.
197   I didn't decide to start self-identifying as a poet until I was 29, and it was the best decision I ever made. Then again, most things are easier to action when you're not depressed. Maybe if I'd been in a better headspace when younger and making my gentle gestures towards hip-hop I could have *made something* of it? Probably not, though. I didn't have the talent.
198   But, alas, no he won't, not really. But once Hip-Scott is dead, Solid Bald will be born. ("The boy is dead, long live the bald.")

Video notes:

Completely different from all other pieces, 'En Toure' evidences the movements I'd made in my non-Hip-Scott writing. There was less crudity and more earnestness, there was more despair and less of a sense of the termination of suffering. Hair loss had been and gone, I had become a demi-vierge, and I felt no optimism. It was a tough time.

Performance Notes:

Quite earnest, self-effacing. It's an interesting document (to me). Some of the rapping is quite slick, some of the spoken word sections have a sense of a genuine emotion. This was Scott Manley Hadley moving, successfully, in a direction that was no longer compatible with Hip-Scott.

Track Rating:

x/5 – I think this is sufficiently different from the rest to render pointless a comparative rating. None of the other ratings are pointless, though, they are all *essential*.

13. XXXMas Special 2 – All I Want For Xmas Is A Wig Made Of My Own Pubes

December 31st, 2013

Lyrics: [199]

[the first 45 seconds of the song include Hip-Scott badly singing Mariah Carey's 'All I Want for Christmas is You', with the final chorus lyric being changed to "hair", instead of "you". The rap is then performed over a midi version of Wu Tang Clan's 'C.R.E.A.M.']

Christmas Rules Everything Around Me,
Elf! Get the turkey! Jesus, baubles, sleigh, yeah!
Christmas Rules Everything Around Me,
Elf! Get the Jesus! Bauble, reindeer, sleigh, yeah!

Hello and I'm hip-hop Santa Claus,
I'm sat reading all my letters in the freezing cold North Pole,
Here's one from a baldie named Scott,
He's wishing for his hair, wants it back up top.[200]

Though I'm magic as Christmas, I can't fix baldness,[201]
But I can give him tips to improve his look.

Do what I do, yeah, and remove your pubes,
Stick them to a bit of plastic using PVA glue,[202]
Put that on your head and dress up in red,
I guarantee straight away you'll start to feel pretty good.

Feel like a person who matters, with hair on your head[203],
As the pubes tickle you on the back of your neck.
Don't be sad because there isn't hair on the top of your scalp,
If there's any on your body, move it up there from somewhere else.[204]

---

199   Several people told me, when I made this, that it was the best thing I'd ever done. No one has said that about anything I've done since, so we must view this, then, as my artistic peak.

200   Hip-Scott began by mentioning baldness, and he ends on it, too.

201   Often, genies and other magical creatures have limits to their power: for example, some magicians cannot bring people back from the dead, some cannot uncook an egg, others cannot time travel, most cannot grant infinite wishes. Here, I imagined the limits of Santa Claus as being unable to cure male pattern baldness. Which is pessimistic.

202   In the accompanying video I do this.

203   This line is significant as it shows the low self-esteem I had by the Winter of 2016. "Feel like a person who matters, with hair on your head" is a very melancholic line. By this point, I had written a few articles about hair loss for Huffington Post, always with a hyperbolic negativity. But I truly believed – as I wrote for Huff Post – that "a bald man in a nightclub is as welcome as a corpse". I hated myself because I was bald. I hated myself because I was depressed. I hated myself because I was bald and depressed. I hated my life because I was still living it. I'm so glad I am no longer there. (Note from Summer 2020: at least, as I sometimes reminisce self-destructively, that unhappy vapid life was *fucking eventful*.)

204   This is, as I well know, the basic procedure for all "hair transplants". Though people joke about moving pubes and bum hair, in reality most of these procedures involve moving follicles from the *side* of the head, which is commonly the last part of the scalp where a baldie loses functional follicles. No citation needed, I'm bald, this is common knowledge to my people.

Christmas Rules Everything Around Me,
Elf! Get the presents! Turkey, brandy, sprouts, yeah!
Christmas Rules Everything Around Me,
Elf! Get the donkey! Angel, Joseph, sleigh, yeah!

[Scott then narrates the slow passage of PVA-covered pubes from the swimming cap on his head down his face and into his mouth. He then nearly throws up, looking utterly pathetic.]

Video notes:

Again, pretty sloppily produced, very domestic, but it is real life footage of me making a wig of pubes on a swimming cap drenched in PVA glue. I'd go so far as to describe this as a masterpiece.

Performance Notes:

Vocally, a clear performance. All of the music is rejigged midi files, so very little could go wrong. Top Hip-Scott. A great place to leave things.

Track Rating:

5/5: Is it self-indulgent? Yes. Is it humiliating? Yes. Is it funny? Yes. Is it really weird? Yes. Tick tick tick tick tick. Hip-Scott is ending on a high. Better this be the end than the documentary.

14. (BONUS) Solid Bald* Theme (Gold-Plated, Bald-Pated)

December 31st, 2013

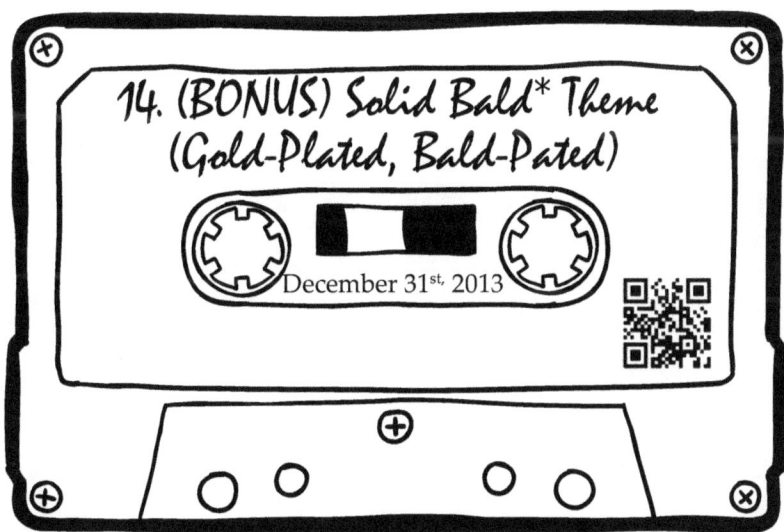

Medley with Black Sabbath's War Pigs

Live at Burley Fisher Books, Dalston

---

*   When Hip-Scott died – probably by choking on a combination of PVA glue and his own pubes – Solid Bald was born. The outfits were more provocative but the body less enticing… The lyrics less crass, but also less amusing. To date, Solid Bald has released three original songs, as well as *lots* of covers (Solid Bald is, essentially, my depressed synth covers band). The lyrics to all three original tracks will be included here.

Lyrics:

Gold-plated, bald-pated,
Gold-plated, it's Solid Bald. [repeat]

Bald-pated but still gold-plated,
Living in a world where hair loss is hated.
Some things that glitter are bald,
Some people get bald before they get old.[205]

Bald but not forgotten, bald to the bone,
My scalp holds power like a rolling stone.
A bald man breathes, a bald man's alive,
A bald man's got a heart with feelings inside.[206]

Took a razor to my head, not my wrists,
Even though I'm bald I have a right to exist.[207]
Bald is beautiful, Bald[208] shines like Gold,
My scalp is strong; I'm Solid Bald.[209]

---

205   Like Scott Manley Hadley aka Hip-Scott aka Solid Bald.
206   Is a lack of emotionality in the bald a commonly-held misconception? Yes.
207   I didn't feel that I had a right to exist when I wrote this lyric, and not just because I was bald, but because I was a bald, unsuccessful person without money or an Oxbridge degree.
208   "Bald" is capitalised in the document where I found these lyrics, and I think it's significant: even though these "bald pride" lyrics manage to perpetuate negative bald stereotypes (i.e. that all bald people are suicidal), the quest for self-confidence is real. Each lyric, each line, demands self-respect, and even though self-respect cannot come from outside, the act of asking for it is a positive step. Maybe.
209   I'm happy with this as a name, because it acknowledges that being bald defines me, but also makes the moniker so extreme that it becomes humorous. Yes, I am bald, yes, I have felt shame because of that, but I do not any longer and I am not going to have this opinion changed. (From Summer 2020: I find my baldness disgraceful.)

Video notes:

The only video performance of this song is from the 20+ minute recording of the launch of *Bad Boy Poet*, my 2018 poetry collection which would go on to be 'Highly Commended' in the Forward Prizes for Poetry 2019. In this portion of the video, I change into a shiny gold tracksuit while hiding in a "changing room" constructed by sellotaping several gold "foil curtains" to a hoop. As I change, the instrumental version of 'Solid Bald Theme (Gold-Plated, Bald-Pated)' plays. I step through the gold curtain and then recite the lyrics in a cod-serious, "performance poet" pastiche. People laugh. It's funny.

Performance Notes:

No known recording exists in which *the lyrics are rapped over the beat,* and though both portions sounded lovely to an audience mostly unaware of the shared oeuvre of Hip-Scott and Solid Bald, to me, as a fan, as a completist, it doesn't count as a "real" performance of 'Solid Bald Theme (Gold-Plated, Bald-Pated)', which was written as a rap piece.

Track Rating:

?/5: it is impossible to judge the quality of something that has never existed **in its truest form**. Though I *love* the beat and I *love* the lyrics, until I hear them combined I will withhold judgement. And if anyone is ever gonna hear them, it's gonna be me.

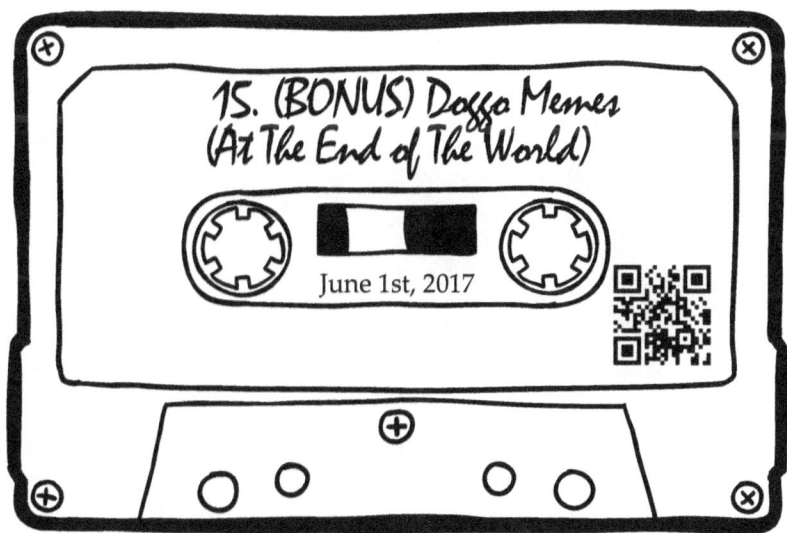

15. (BONUS) Doggo Memes
(At The End of The World)

June 1st, 2017

Lyrics: 210 211

I know what you like, I know what you believe to be
The cultural highlight of all humanity.
The thing that always makes you smile,
Yes, I'm talking [a]bout those doggo memes.

But if they disappeared, if the whole internet broke down,
If all of the doggos and puppers and pupperinos ran away from every town,
In a world without cameras and screens,
I'd recreate the doggo memes for you.

I'd dress as a doggo, and I know I don't have any hair
But I would find some and stick it to my head, palms, tummy, my feet and everywhere;
I'd make big ears out of the cardboard boxes fallout shelters come in,
To recreate the doggo memes for you.

I'd learn all the jargon, I'd scratch it into my skin,
Because in this dystopia without internet, dogs and pictures there wouldn't be papers & pen,
So I could look like a doggo,
And know the words for the doggo memes.

I would say:[212] doggo, bamboozle, heckin, pupper, snoot, boof, fren, nugget and bork,
And I'd say schmako, angery, and ohai, and hooman, and halp and a borf,
If we both survived the end of civilisation as we know it,
I'd still do doggo memes for you.

---

210   One of the three Solid Bald original songs (to date), 'Doggo Memes (At The End of the World)' was written as a love song during the end of my former long term, mutually unsatisfying, relationship. I think it is significant that the only possible scenario in which I could imagine exhibiting emotional care to my then-partner was a post-apocalyptic one. "If the world ended, if society collapsed, *then* I could envisage trying to cater to your emotional needs", is what I was saying. It was mutually negative, mutually destructive. Any words in the following lyrics that are unfamiliar were part of the – now defunct – set of memes that were popular for a bit between like 2015 and 2017.

211   Due to some kind of shame, I imagine, I only ever released this song as part of an episode of my unsuccessful 2017 web series, #TotNTV. I didn't love the person I wrote this love song for, I just didn't believe I could *survive* without them. "The best revenge is to live well" is a popular phrase now, and I *am* living well by my own standards, however *my* standards are *vastly* different from most people's.

212   This is, I believe, an exhaustive list of "doggo meme" jargon.

I would say: doggo, bamboozle, heckin, pupper, snoot, boof, fren, nugget
and bork,
And I'd say schmako, angery, and ohai, and hooman, and halp and a borf,
If we both survived the end of the world,
I'd do the doggo memes for you.

If we both survived the end of civilisation as we know it,
I'd still do doggo memes for you.

If we outlived the internet,
I'd do doggo memes for you.

Video notes:

Performed as "Solid Bald", a sequinned, gold, depressed cabaret singer. Solid Bald swings a wooden tulip around like a cheese-eating Morrissey, and the strip lights reflect off his sequins. It is simple and understated and as close to an expression of a dead love as Scott Manley Hadley could manage.

Performance notes:

I like the tune, still, and I think Solid Bald delivers most lines with clarity. However, I clearly hadn't learnt the subculture-specific jargon that was meant to be the finale of the song, which is telling about the falsity of the premise. There seems to be pain here. Performing a desperate love song without love, a love song that could only imagine positive love after the end of the world. Absolutely fucking bleak. I was not well.

Track rating:

It might be worth me digging this out of retirement and recording a version detoxified from its psychological burden. I won't, though. It exists, as it is, as a testament to the end of something bad. I like that, maybe. 5/5

16. (BONUS) Wet Dog

January 27th 2018

Lyrics:

I'm A Wet Dog,
I'm A Wet Dog,
I'm A Wet Dog,
I am A Wet Dog.

Walking on the street with no shoes on your feet
That's a dog's life, yeah, and it ain't sweet.
Got a fur coat on but it's stuck to my skin,
So when it starts to rain it's like I'm sewed in.

If my fur gets wet then so do I,
When water starts falling straight outta the sky,
It gets all over my legs, all over my hair,
There's nowhere to hide if you're nude everywhere.

Being a dog, no it ain't easy.
Being a dog, not good when it's breezy.
Being a dog, it's bad in the cold.
Being a dog, you gotta eat food from a bowl.

Try drying yourself without using a towel,
Try digging a hole without using a trowel,
Try going peepee outside in the rain,
Try being walked on a lead without feeling any pain.

You wouldn't like it, being a dog,
To be a good boy, yeah, you gotta be tough.
You gotta go outside whatever the weather,
You gotta poo in the street even when it's wet, yeah.

[repeat chorus]

Video notes:

A simple video, shot in Leicestershire while walking from a station to the boatyard where I bought the structurally-unsound boat that lost me thousands of pounds[213]. At least I got this simple music video featuring Cubby playing in a field out of it.

Performance Notes:

Simple musically, but the lyrics are clear. It's family friendly rap from the perspective of a dog. Scott Manley Hadley has changed. It's odd to see. More hope, maybe. More antidepressants. A little bit of Valium.

Track Rating:

4/5 – does exactly what it sets out to do. It's uncomplex.

---

213   See annotation to the lyric "never lived on the streets" in the song 'Born To Rap'.

17. (EXCLUSIVE) I'm A Rapper
2018 REMIX: I'm A Poet

November 16th 2018

Lyrics:[214]

[chorus]   *I'm A Poet*
                    yes, I'm a bad boy poet

                    I'm A Poet
                    yes, I'm a bad boy poet

                    I'm A Poet
                    yes, I'm a bad boy poet

                    I'm A Poet
                    Yes…
                    I'm a bad boy poet

I'm a fresh new poet, I'm new to the scene
And I'm the best bad boy poet that there's ever fucking been.
I don't glamorise drugs, sex or rhyme schemes,
Well how'd I write such poetic wet dreams?

Well, my poetry's mature, my poetry's grown-up,
I write my verse in Calibri, not by hand in a note-book.
I'm not young, but I'm not old school,
I know who I am and I'm an adult, fool.

I'm mature like wine, I don't smell like cheese,
My poems bring the penitent up off their knees
Cuz they think I'm the brand new verse messiah
Cuz I write poems more fiery than a funeral pyre.

I'm angry, I'm sharp, I'm poetically gifted,
You can see the gold in my verse without having to sift it,
Google my nudes, I don't scrub up too badly,
There's no better bad boy poet than Scott Manley Hadley.

[repeat chorus]

I make a bit of love, but don't make a lot of cash,
It's probably for the best, I'm already too brash.
I write poems when I wake up, I write poems when I sleep,
I even write poems when I'm cleaning my motherfucking teeth.

---

214   To see the original lyrics of this track, flick back a few pages.

Some people try to tell me I write poems too much,
Well you people, you can just fuck off:
Poems for me is like breathing for you,
It's not a hobby it's something that I *have to do*.

Probably rather chop my balls off than give it up
What's the point in shaggin' if you can't type it up?
My poems are a gift to the whole fucking world,
Everyone's talking about them, haven't you heard?

From London to Paris, Black Mountain to Berkeley,
The hot shots of the verse world know they gotta be ready.
Rupi Kaur called me up, she said, "I'd blurb your book gladly,
There's no better bad boy poet than Scott Manley Hadley."[215]

[repeat chorus]

How many poems have I got within me,
Well, my soul is bottomless poetry,
There're so many more poems for me to write,
Get out the disinfectant, cuz this is hot shite.[216]

Every poem I write is like a mental explosion,
The world's going mad with a Christ-like devotion,
I'm just a poet, guys, cool it all down,
I can't help being the most badass poet in this fucking town.

But don't despair, with practice you can be like me,
I didn't write poems 'til I was nearly thirty,
And now I'm so fucking fly I feel like a Boeing,
I'm touching the sky like it got money owing.[217]

---

215   Rupi Kaur did not call me up, in fact all of the people who blurbed *Bad Boy Poet* are people
I have huge respect for. I have never read an entire book of Kaur's work, but I have been consistently
unimpressed by her poetry whenever I've encountered it organically. I should probably read a collection to
gain an informed opinion and it might turn out that I like it. Also, obviously, given Kaur's fame and success,
if she offered to blurb my book I'd discard everyone else immediately. It's lovely to have affirmation from
great writers, but it's more remunerative to have affirmation from *popular* writers. I'd love to be rich enough
to feed my dog an entire organic, cornfed, chicken every day, and that will never happen if I remain as poor
as the writers I actually like, lol. No offence if any of you are reading this.
216   Is this a deliberate attempt to refer back to 'En Toure'? I doubt it.
217   Uncertain why this lyric survived the editing process.

My poems are gorgeous, I'm writing fresh magic,
To continue with planes, I'm Virgin Atlantic.
My verse is so hot it burns crazy madly,
There's no better bad boy poet than Scott Manley Hadley.

[repeat chorus until the world ends]

Video notes:

This is again a live performance from the *Bad Boy Poet* launch, held in the basement of Burley Fisher Books, Dalston, London, England. I flew in from Barcelona just for the launch. So fucking jet-set. I had a long day traversing London back and forth to visit independent book shops with Sean Preston, the Publisher at Open Pen, so by the end of the evening I was tired and stressed. I'm making excuses for myself, and that's because:

Performance notes:

The performance is absolutely fucking atrocious. Though it's not quite as bad as the live version of 'Pass The Dostoevsky On The Left Hand Side' (which begins off-key and remains so for most of the track), I frequently forget the lyrics and drop out of rhythm. This doesn't even boast the nudity I gift the audience in the performance of 'Pass The Dostoevsky...' (I return to the previously-mentioned "changing room" and remove all clothes before changing into a sequined leotard) which means that here, like in many of my music videos and recordings – the *performance doesn't do justice to a stellar, evergreen, track.*

Track rating:

BUT... it's so good that the power of the song-writing and the passion of the lyrics transcends their piss-poor interpretation. This song is something of which I, as a rapper, remain truly, truly proud. 5/5.

Closing Thoughts

Hip-Scott was *horny*.

Hip-Scott was a vocal space for me to accidently reveal serious personal problems.

I stopped using the name Hip-Scott because I wanted something less self-effacing, less self-mocking.

Solid Bald is self-celebratory, Hip-Scott was self-hating.

Maybe these bad raps should be removed from the internet; maybe this overlong text (lol it's actually a book now haha) shouldn't exist. But this *does* exist (unless I'm hallucinating it, which isn't impossible), and likewise *the happier individual I now am* would not exist without the lyrical, performative and creative mis-decisions I made when younger.

Hip-Scott's flawed honesty helped me to become a better person.

Doing something badly that I enjoyed doing allowed me to focus on learning to *do well* things that mattered (to me) more.[218]

I'm the happiest I've ever been at the moment. And maybe that won't last, but if it doesn't, I'll always have the music.[219] Because I am Scott Manley Hadley aka Solid Bald aka Hip-Scott and, to quote myself:

I'm a rapper.
Yes.
I'm a motherfucking rapper.

---

218   I'm referring to my poetry, a bit arrogantly tbh.
219   Spoiler alert from Summer 2020: the happiness didn't last.

Production Notes

All tracks produced, recorded and mastered by Scott Manley Hadley aka Solid Bald aka Hip-Scott.

All music composed and performed by Scott Manley Hadley except Track 11 (written by Joan Javits & Philip Springer, music performed by Garage Band midi reader), Track 13 ('All I Want For Christmas Is You' written by Mariah Carey & Walter Afanasieff; 'C.R.E.A.M' written by Robert Diggs, Jason Hunter, Clifford Smith & Corey Woods; both performed by Garage Band midi reader) and Track 10 (written by Ben Haggerty, Thomas Bangalter, Guy-Manuel de Homem-Christo, Nile Rodgers, Pharrell Williams, Robin Thicke, Clifford Harris Jr., Lukasz Gottwald, Maureen "Mozella" McDonald, Kiyanu Kim, Stephan Moccio, Sacha Skarbek & Henry Walter, performed by Scott Manley Hadley).

All music videos directed and edited by Scott Manley Hadley. Additional filming by Lauren [Manley] Hadley & Dr. Jane Frances Dunlop. Apologies if anyone else helped me do any of this and I've forgotten, but I think this has been pretty onanistic from the start.

Except where indicated, all notes were written in Barcelona, Catalunya, in Summer 2018.

Appendices

Appendix A
selection of illuminating poems written by scott manley hadley in Summer 2020

On the second or third date
At the start of the
Longest relationship I've ever had
My then-girlfriend asked
If I was bisexual.
I laughed
And said no.

But
I felt like I was lying
To her and to myself
And that I was waiting
For a real man to fix me
(like James Bond and Pussy Galore)
And that I wasn't heterosexual
I was instead
incredibly
fucking
repressed.

As the decades rush on
I realise
Yes,
Maybe
That was
Right.

///

when i'm alone now
i refer to myself now
as non-binary now
and then
when I'm about to tell my lover
i think
maybe it's the bpd

i look like a man
i'm bald like a man
i have a dick like a man
but i don't feel like a man

this is what i'm thinking about
this is why
i cannot talk
i cannot write
i have no authentic self

///

the parts inside of me
do not make a whole

there is enough
and not enough
to go round

i have questions
poems can't answer

///

I am not enjoying my life,
So I scratch my own arm with a knife.
When I look in the mirror,
I do a whole body shiver,
I'll never be someone's beautiful wife.

Appendix B

My high school non-friend, [name redacted], as fictionalised in White Lines, Black Truffles, an unpublished "Catholic cocaine novel" written by Scott Manley Hadley in 2012, while holding down a full-time office job and partying every weekend.

[name redacted] was a guy I went to school with. Never my friend. I knew him, yeah, sure. If I'd pass him on the street we wouldn't blank each other, but nor would we stop to chat. It's not that he was *cooler* than me (though I'm sure he thought that he was and I, at the time, *definitely* saw myself as cooler than him), we just moved in very different circles. In and outside of school. He was one of the big drug users, big weed smokers, from a young age. From year nine, maybe even year eight, onwards, he'd come into school stoned every morning. He'd never been intellectually gifted, but whatever his grades had been as a *child*, they were certainly less impressive as he became a teenager and, later, a young adult. I don't know if he went to University. I don't know if he'd have got the grades necessary to go to University. I don't know much about him. Never did. He was part of the chavvy drug-taking set, the group that lived in the town we all went to school in rather than one of the villages nearby. The other drug-taking set, the one that I'd have considered "cool" (though I was far from being part of it and many years from being a regular drug user) was the hippyish, bohemian, liberal clique. They'd all dress in silly clothes, drink cider in parks next to museums, openly smoke marijuana; they'd hang around in a mixed-gender group and discuss films and books and music. A lot of them were in bands. Sexually active, politically opinionated, (most) reasonably well off. They made drug use aspirational.

[name redacted] was not part of that group.

He'd get stoned in the mornings, the lunch break, the afternoons, the evenings, with boys who went to the rougher high school the other end of town. They all had short hair, dressed in tracksuits and there were constant (never proven) rumours that they carried knives. [name redacted] was a bit dodgy. Played the drums (quite well), but though he used to hang around with the trendier, artsier kids at gigs, he always seemed more comfortable with his primary school friends. He is the only man I have ever punched in the face.

Between finishing school and where I am now – 25, single, unemployed, living with my parents (No. It's been a fortnight since I left London. A fortnight. That's all.) – I've had no contact with [name redacted]. We are Facebook friends, so occasionally he'll pop up (used to pop up) on my newsfeed, often with announcements of gigs he's playing at or going to see. Heavy metal and drum and bass were his genres of choice as a teenager. I remember that. He posts "memes" featuring jokes about drugs. Constantly. A picture of a toddler in snow and a caption pretending it's cocaine, a poorly photoshopped image of a politician with a spliff, things like that. Daily. He clearly thinks they're funny. Which, to my desperate, judgemental, hypocritical mind, implied that he probably still had ready access to marijuana. Which was the link I planned to use.

[...[220]]

Al fresco, in the Swan car park, I realised the ridiculousness of the situation. The beer garden had a complete view of where I was stood. A broad daylight drug deal in a public place suddenly seemed a stupid thing to have agreed to. Maybe the ease with which this had happened was a sign, a warning. Maybe it *was* too easy, a setup? Maybe [name redacted] had rejected drug-use post-school, become police and started chasing down his old friends and acquaintances still partial to the good stuff? Maybe he was going to mug me and not even give me the weed. Leave me sober, robbed and bleeding behind a factory in the industrial estate round the corner?

The knife wounds I was mentally picturing were decimated by:

'Paul fucking Simmons?'

I span on the gravel, a Michael Jackson pirouette.

'[name redacted].'

---

220   In the narrative interim, Paul Simmons (basically me but less sexually repressed, with a better job and – the most significant difference – a fan of marijuana) has been shopping in a Waitrose after arranging to meet [name redacted] in a pub carpark to purchase some cannabis. Paul is staying with his teacher parents in a barely fictionalised version of the town I went to school in, rather than my own native Redditch which – as we've learned earlier in this book – has "no connections, no Waitrose". Paul has returned to his hometown to detox after the throbbing Catholic guilt he felt for his decadent life of sex and drugs (and other fun things) overwhelmed him. He threw his iPhone in the Thames. It's that kind of novel. Whenever I dip back into the manuscript I genuinely find it hilarious, but I don't think it works as a piece because the satire is diminished by an absence of consequence by the novel's end. It reads as a piece of propaganda *lauding* amorality, rather than as a piece attacking it. The first draft came in at 160,000 words. Good times.

His arms were wide, as was the grin plastered across his round face. He was one of those people who, though never overweight, had chubby cheeks and was always incorrectly categorised as fat. His teeth were yellowing. As were his fingertips. He was smoking a cigarette, a straight, wearing a black T-shirt with a band I'd never heard of on it. The sleeves were short, rolled up over surprisingly impressive biceps, his faded jeans loose around the waist, and cut in a style fashionable when we were teenagers. Good jeans worn for too long. Shoes: stained Reeboks. His hair short, blonde. Glasses, not the faux-NHS style everyone I knew preferred; [name redacted] wore thin-framed, classic Specsavers. He was gawping. He looked genuinely pleased to see me. Or at least genuinely pleased to see me under these circumstances.

We shook hands, slapped each other's backs. A greeting far more personal than the last time we'd seen each other. People feel more connected, wistful, positive, about their youth the older they get. And at this messy stage of life, the last illusions of being young, having a future, potential, success to look forward to but exuberance and selfishness and hedonism to enjoy... at this messy stage one finds it tough to self-categorise. Am I a man or am I a boy? What is [name redacted]? He still lives where we went to school. He still plays in a band. He still dresses like a teenager. Maybe he takes more powerful narcotics, maybe he has a girlfriend, a job, maybe his parents have health issues, maybe things are going great, maybe he's sad, disappointed, maybe he's... maybe I should've asked first.

'How're you, man? Long fucking time, long fucking...' he took a drag on his cigarette. 'You walk or drive?'

'I drove, and I'm-'

'Sweet, man, sweet. Let's hop in. What's your motor?'

He scanned the car park, I pointed at the battered Ford.

'You're fucking joking, that shitheap?'

Shitheap? 'It's my Dad's.'

He sneered at the rust as he opened the passenger door. 'Fucking teachers' wages, ey?'

He laughed as we closed the doors.

'Let's go for a drive, yeah? Use the bypass, go round that way.'

He didn't put on a seatbelt, so I didn't either, and we drove across the gravel and into the road, taking a left at the immediate roundabout onto the dual carriageway. Trying to look cool, I jacked the speed up to seventy as quickly as the car would let me. As I changed my mind and nervously clipped my seatbelt into place, [name redacted] asked again how I was.

'I'm good, I'm good. I'm OK. Between jobs and women at the moment, you know, so... err... thought I'd come and scrounge off the folks for a bit.' Fuck. That isn't how I talk. 'Yourself?'

'Fuckin' A, fuck-king _A_, man. My band's doin' good, lot of gigs, you should come down, work's good, took up as a mechanic, you know, so... good money, good wage. Got a better fuckin' motor than this anyway, hahaha. And I've got a right fit girlfriend as well. You remember Dani from our class?'

Vaguely, but if he means who I think he does, she was far from good-looking. 'Yeah.'

'Yeah, well, her younger sister. Youngest sister, yeah. Fuckin' twenty-one, tightest fuckin' twat I've had in years, you know what I mean? Hahaha. I'm joking, a bit, like, proper tart, yeah, but I'm still fuckin' old enough to notice the difference. Hahaha.'

You smile, realising that despite your love of fucking women, you've never got into the habit of comparing vaginal tightness. It's almost odd, that for all of your and Jake's recent proclivity towards explicit conversational descriptions of personal sexual experience, this isn't something you mention. The widespread, casual, nod to feminism of the middle-classes. The heterosexual guilt. Trying not to *intellectually* objectify women, but all the while fantasising, fucking, fingering, licking and staring at them as if they were objects. Saying one wouldn't, shouldn't, couldn't, doesn't, do that kind of thing, but pumping a rock hard cock over the thought of a sweaty pair of tits you saw in a park is hardly fucking suffragette behaviour.

'Where were you living? Up in Brum?'

You know you've come a long way from London when other British cities are considered liveable options.

'No, no, down in London. Work in Sales.'

'Sweet. What kinda stuff?'

'Oh, it was...' I can't be fucked. 'Corporate stuff, fucking tax avoidance. Boring. Dry. 'Swhy I got out.'

'Nice. Money good?'

'Yeah, money was good, yeah, I'll fuckin' miss that.' Let's drop some consonants. 'But I think I can get the same or more doing something a bit more... more fun, yeah, you know?'

We were approaching the roundabout that marked the end of the dual carriageway. 'Which way?'

'Wherever, man. Just somewhere without CCTV, you know? My ket dealer got fuckin' three years 'cause some factory forecourt camera got him selling to a guy in a car. Fuckin' moron. The pigs are fuckin' tryin' to lock it all down. I reckon they're stockpiling for a fucking megalash, the little piggies'll fuckin' hoover up anything they can get their hands on. My ex bird used to, she told me, like, said she used to suck off this guy she knew, and they'd just get fucking mashed, you know, on ching and pills and shit, you know, just knew him from long back, yeah, and it turned out he was a cop. Could fuckin' put it away, my, like, ex-missus said, yeah, and I said does 'e put this away as well as I do, like his cock' (he pointed) 'you know. She fuckin' cracked up. Great girl. Moved to Norwich, like, for the canals.'

I didn't know what to say but [name redacted] seems keen to avoid silence.

'You're not the first old boy to contact me for fuckin' weed recently, you know. That fuckin', that fuckin'... what's 'e called... the, you know, the, the, the...' he was clicking his fingers and screwing up his face into the tightest ball of concentration I'd ever seen on anyone over five. It worked. 'Fuckin' Jack Robinson, like? You remember, the fuckin', the fuckin'... the fuckin' pianist, yeah? Well, it turns out he was like touring with some fuckin', some fuckin' show, like, and banged this fuckin' girl bareback in like, fuckin' Switzerland or somewhere and even though she said she was like on the coil or whatever she got up the duff from this like backstage shag and now he has this kid in Switzerland and he said he just has to send all his money to her and the kid and so he's had to stop like playin' piano and start workin' in some fuckin' office to pay the child support. Poor guy. Poor fuckin' guy.'

There was a pause.

'I always presumed he was gay.'

[name redacted] snorted with laughter, hooted, screamed, grabbed his sides, rolled in the seat.

Once he'd calmed down: 'You're thinkin' of Jake Robertson.' He wiped a tear from his eye. A huge, cat-like grin. 'Robinson woulda fuckin' decked you for that.'

Appendix C

an excerpt from The Body and the Baptist, *an attempt at popular historical fiction written by Scott Manley Hadley while completing an MA in Creative & Life Writing, 2013-2014*

It is many months later and the carpenter has returned from the wilderness. Today he stands near the freshwater sea of his homeland.

He has an audience.

Men and women sit on the rocks around the water's edge, legs dangling in. Shaded by willow trees, there is a gentle breeze that moves their robes. Eyes look towards a man who stands (the only one who stands), a few feet away, *on the soil.* He is a Galilean carpenter newly come to prominence amongst those who speak of God. Unlike the Baptist, he speaks in plain language of plain people: of good people praised, of bad people redeemed. Unlike the Baptist, he enjoys a glass of wine, is rumoured to be married (though no one has seen his wife) and takes pride in his appearance. Unlike the Baptist, he has managed to retain the relaxing disposition of youth since beginning his ministry. Unlike the Baptist, he speaks of *today.*

Be good for the bounty of the world to come, he preaches, *But be good, too, because you desire goodness in your life.*

The two preachers share some ideas. They both believe that every man can be saved if he repents. Every woman can be saved, too, the Galilean thinks, but this is not something the Baptist would agree with. He ignores the female like he ignores the king. He speaks to a part of his audience outside reality. He talks of the infinite, of a future there is no guarantee will ever come to pass. The Baptist begs men to be clean for a meeting with God, yet fails to teach how they may find God within themselves.

And this is where the younger preacher's strength lies. His allegories and fables do more than the Baptist's impassioned proclamations, because rather than advocating suffering and pain until death, the Galilean teaches his listeners to see the eternal in the everyday. All men, all women, are in every parable. The lowest born, the lowest fallen, can rise to become the holiest seen. This message is what pulls attention to him. The Baptist said, once, *We must preach to all, but a temple filled with lepers and whores will keep the majority away.*

But that isn't true. A temple open to lepers and whores is a temple open to *everyone*. No one has fallen too far to be redeemed. No one is too unclean to be touched. Now, the Galilean isn't preaching guiltless promiscuity, as one of the more radical groups in the desert allegedly is, but he *is* preaching compassion, consideration, affection, for all. His message is universal.

He speaks with a loud voice, but never a shout, offering wit and love to a crowd:

Each of you is God's child and he loves you and will forgive your sins. God is our father, our protector and our judge. If we offend him – and offend him we must, for it is human nature for children to offend their parents – we must acknowledge our sins and apologise. We should do this, too, to people we offend: if you raise your voice to your wife or child or friend, apologise.

Love God and – as you love God – love the people who surround you. For God is love, and without God there would be no love.

Love God, yes, and love God because it is by his grace that you have children and warmth and food and wine and beautiful plants and this sea full of fish and parents when we are children and husbands and wives when we are adults.

Love those you see every day: love the man who sells you fish, love the child your son invites to play who knocks over a bowl of water, love the man who collects your taxes, love the woman who tells you she wishes she were married to your husband. Love the person who lives next door, love everyone you pass in the street, for God is love, and the most divine way to honour him is by bringing love to the world in ever increased doses. Each instance of love is a silent prayer.

The Galilean, stood on a rock, holds his arms wide and offers a life of happiness and peace and pleasure. He says:

God created seas and valleys and lakes. He created us and the animals and plants we must consume to live. But with that comes the knowledge that God created wine, meat and beauty. God created pleasures and pleasant objects for us to enjoy. Music and song and wine and poetry are fine ways to honour God, because they are fine ways to honour each and everything in existence. A fine fish, cooked over a fire and enjoyed between a family, a mother, a father, children, a grandparent if God has blessed them with long life, is a prayer; to enjoy the flavours he created in food with our mouths he created able to enjoy them is an act of love to God. To enjoy any part of his creation is to love it, to enjoy anything without harming another is never a sin: it is what he hopes for us to do. And another thing... Here he always lowers his voice, *God created sex.* Often those who listen start to giggle. *Adultery may be a sin, but because it separates sex from love, it involves lies and hatred and disloyalty. But when a husband and a wife send their children to play outside, close the doors and spend some time making another one... When two people who know each other's bodies inside out spend some time getting a little bit of outside in –* for some reason this euphemism always makes people laugh – *there is no sin in that. And when you grip each other afterwards, not wanting to move because the intimacy is perfect – how is that a sin? Why would God make our bodies so capable of joy if he didn't want us to enjoy them?* He then points at the oldest person present, man or woman, and says, *[He/she] knows what I'm talking about!* which always provokes great laughter and the carpenter grins sheepishly as the man or woman blushes and covers his or her face, or smiles widely at a spouse if present.

People have a good time with the Galilean. Audiences leave feeling happier and holier and, like they did when leaving the speeches of the Baptist at his most popular, a little bit turned on. But turned on to the joys of marital sex, to the acceptable and the familiar, the comfortable and the known. The Galilean reckons the big caravans that returned to Jerusalem after the Baptist's speeches probably detoured via a brothel. But he encourages people to go to their own bed.

If God is love – and he is – then the act of love is an act of God. When you come with the one you love, you are reaching a prayer to God.

Think about that when the light gets dim, he closes with, often accompanied by a wink.

Appendix D: 'death bed'

poem cycle written 2018-2019 about the death by cancer of Scott Manley Hadley's maternal grandmother in 2014

I still think about my nan dying
Many years on.

Not her death
Not the circumstance of her death (cancer)
But her
Dying
As a human,
As a woman,
As my nan.

She died in her home
A safe
Place
In the downstairs front room
That had always before
Functioned as
A dining room.

In place of the table
(at which I sat
For every family Christmas
From my birth
To her death)
Was a hospital bed
Hired for as long
As it would take her to die.

The room was cleared
Of its bookshelves
And crockery
Of its cutlery
And chairs
And instead
Of family dinners
We gathered there
For death.

///

I ate a lot of radishes that summer.

I don't know why my granddad kept buying them
Panicking
In the supermarket
Not knowing
What to provide
For your children
And grandchildren
Visiting
Your dying wife.

Maybe
If I hadn't eaten the radishes
He wouldn't have bought more
Because I don't remember them
From before
And I don't think
I've seen them
In his house
Since.

///

My nan
Couldn't eat solid food,
For more than the last week.

She drank protein shakes
Like a weightlifter
But instead
Of bulking up
The muscle fell
From her face.

My cousin
Who had just learnt to drive
Brought my nan a McDonalds milkshake
I don't remember the flavour
But I do remember

The way she sucked it
While he held it
Then as soon as he was out the room
She stretched out
And it fell
To the floor.

Did she do it on purpose
Because she was too sick
To drink it
But too polite
To reject
The gift?

I think so
But I will never know.

I think the flavour
was banana.

///

Lying on the hospital bed
In her own front room
Dying in front of daytime television
White sheets kept washed
Changed by nurses twice a day
Who changed the nappies they put on her too.

Her skin withered
Her bones rose
And the cancer cancer cancer
Sucked "my nan" out of the woman
Who had always been "my nan".

The nurses moved her
To stop the bedsores
But she was in so much pain
Inside
Why would she care about
A little pain
Outside?

No one let her overdose
On the morphine she was given
Which maybe was what she wanted.

And no one let me find it either
Because they knew
I would've had it
Too.

///

I said to her
Before I left
"Thank you, nan, for everything"
And she gripped my hand
And we nodded our goodbyes
And I left her to death
And she left me
To my unhappy life.

This would have been
A perfect goodbye:
My thanks,
Her lucid enough
To understand.

But she lasted
A few more weeks
And I saw her two more times
And now
When I think about my nan
It is the weakened shell
I picture
When she could no longer
Smile
Laugh
Or properly stay awake.

Hers was the first
Significant death of my life
And seeing her
Wasting away in a

Familiar familial place
Troubled me.

In fact,
It troubles me still.

Though she is not *gone*
Because I still think of her,
But when I do
I do not remember her younger and healthy and alive,
I remember her dying
Fading
Grey
Her arms just skin
Even her bones
Looked brittle and weak.

///

As more time passes
I dream of that Summer more.
For me, it was a time of transitions
And for my nan it was as well.

I do not think
She died in peace
Because I know she believed in God
And I think she felt herself a sinner.

Maybe if she'd lived longer
We could've become close
Because I too
Regret
So much.

///

The next time I visit
My grandad
The bed is gone,
The front room
Back to how it was.

My nan's absence
Stands present
In every room
And I keep turning
Expecting her
To be there.

My granddad talks about
Moving house
Until I excuse myself
To cry.

I stand in the room my nan died in
And I do not see
The table and chairs
I see that bed
But even then
It is empty.

Acknowledgements

Thank you to Aaron and the rest of the Broken Sleep team for publishing this strange, personal, book. Thank you for reading it, I hope you got something out of it.

LAY OUT YOUR UNREST

Broken Sleep Records

www.ingramcontent.com/pod-product-compliance
Lightning Source LLC
LaVergne TN
LVHW041223080426
835508LV00011B/1055